THE DOCTRINE OF THE
CHRISTIAN MINISTRY

THE DOCTRINE
OF THE
CHRISTIAN MINISTRY

by

JOHN LINE

Emmanuel College
University of Toronto
Canada

LUTTERWORTH PRESS
LONDON

CONTENTS

CHAPTER

PAGE

Introduction   7

1   THE DOCTRINE OF APOSTOLIC EPIS-
    COPAL SUCCESSION   11

2   SCRIPTURAL AND HISTORICAL FOUNDA-
    TIONS OF THE DOCTRINE OF APOSTOLIC
    EPISCOPAL SUCCESSION   38

3   EXAMINATION OF THE DOCTRINE OF
    APOSTOLIC EPISCOPAL SUCCESSION   86

4   THE DOCTRINE OF THE MINISTRY: A
    STATEMENT FOR THE CHURCH TODAY   124

    SUMMARY: THE DOCTRINE OF THE
    MINISTRY   179

    Index of Scripture References   185

    General Index   190

INTRODUCTION

THE problem of the Church's Ministry is one that, in ecclesiastical discussions throughout the world, is coming more and more into the foreground.

This is partly because, in the efforts of the Churches to come together, in the ecumenical movement or in plans for formal reunion, it has become apparent that it is in connection with the Ministry and questions cognate to it that the chief—one could almost say all—the hindrances to unity have arisen. Leaders of the Churches repeatedly assert that there is nothing to keep them apart in their basic beliefs, in what they profess concerning God, Christ and the Holy Spirit, the divine provision of Salvation, Resurrection and the Future Life. The representatives of the Churches assembled at Lausanne, in 1927, agreed to declare: "We are united in a common Christian Faith proclaimed in Holy Scripture and witnessed to and safeguarded in the Ecumenical Creed, commonly called the Nicene, and in the Apostles' Creed, which Faith is continually confirmed in the spiritual experience of the Church of Christ."[1] Dr. Nathaniel Micklem wrote in 1943: "There is not, and there never has been, any controversy between the Church of England and Orthodox Dissent in respect of the articles of the Christian Faith"; and Archbishop William Temple endorsed these words in commending the book in which they occurred.[2] Testimonies of this sort could be multiplied. The Churches are divided though the Faith they hold is one. The Doctrine of the Ministry and of the Ordinances is the ground of division. Divergences here that are deep and far-reaching jostle with an impressive accord on the great and central beliefs.

---

[1] Lausanne Conference on Faith and Order, 1927, *Report of Section VI*.
[2] Micklem, *The Doctrine of our Redemption:* the Archbishop's Introduction.

7

When we say questions "cognate to" that of the Ministry we have in mind the differing views held among Christians regarding the Church and the Sacraments. These belong to the problem of the Ministry in that one of the major conflicts is about whether Church and Sacrament require for their true or full nature the presence and ministration of certain orders of Ministers. The discussion of the Ministry evokes this issue or others similar to it at every stage.

It is natural to feel—who has not felt with acute impatience!—that these matters of Form and Order loom disproportionately in current theological writing and ecclesiastical debate. What are they to a world "weary of its pain", distraught from apprehension, uncertain not about Church forms but of God Himself, scanning anxiously for tokens that He lives and cares? This disquiet over the ways of theology is not to be dismissed. One picks up, for example, the volume *Intercommunion*,[1] prepared for the Lund Conference on Faith and Order, 1952, and becomes engrossed; then breaks off to read in the newspaper of the world's current troubles. Where is the connecting equation? A world torn by hate and strife; yearning for peace yet fearful even in doing so of the embarrassments, economic and other, should peace become over-certain. What meaning have the refinements of interchurch dissension shown in this book for the men caught under this strain? What does it offer to mankind's jeopardized existence that the Churches have revealed with nicer precision their variant notions about Rite and its authentic celebration?

Surely it is not this the times are asking of the Churches; instead it all seems unconscionable trifling in face of the distresses and fears and necessities that now stalk the world. Let the Churches awake to their prophetic calling and to the need for more forthrightness in their moral witness. Yet, as we shall see, men in the various Churches hold their beliefs concerning Church and Ministry with strong and devout conviction; and so far from seeing the issues of the Ministry as secondary to those which present world

[1] Baillie and Marsh (eds.).

8

dilemmas lay on the Church's conscience, they discern in the Church's call these two made one. The Church must face her world task, but as the Church, with certainty of her strength and of the fount of her authority; in no wise doubtful that her Ministry is empowered of God.

> If the Church is to go forward, conquering and to conquer in this troubled world, she must go forward as an instrument divinely forged, inspired and maintained, and with the consciousness that this is her true nature. And it is only as she can claim that her Ministry derives direct from the Lord Himself . . . that she can pursue her pilgrimage undaunted.[1]

To those who uphold this outlook upon Church and Ministry, the Church's own structure and offices and her mission to the time are not separate themes. Such is the bond between them, so inwrought is the Church's historical and human purpose with her comprehension of her divine subsistence and ground, that anything which helps this comprehension or in slightest measure makes clearer to the Church the high credential and sign under which her Servants stand will not appear as deflecting the Church from her temporal warfare, or as muffling the charge which through the tensions and upheavals of the age God is bringing to her; but rather as girding her and making her the readier to march with confident step in the way He commands.

Two things have been mentioned in this Introduction that we shall have in mind as we proceed: the desire for the closer unity of the Christian forces; the new focusings of the Church's responsibility in our critical day. Our persuasion is that a proper understanding of the Church's Ministry would afford something to both.

The order in this work is as follows:

1. We shall begin by considering, in the first chapter, the doctrine of Apostolic Episcopal Succession, the belief that the ministry of bishops is traceable back to the Apostles, and is the order and channel through which the Apostolic

[1] The Editor, in *The Apostolic Ministry*, Kirk (ed.) and others, p. 52.

Ministry is transmitted and secured to the Church age by age. Our reason for beginning in this way is that, amid so much thinking on the Ministry that fails to crystallize into a definite doctrine, this belief stands out as definitive and positive, and by way of it we soon come to the questions pertaining to the Ministry that are foremost in ecumenical and other interest.

2. In our next section, we shall trace the origin and emergence of this doctrine and inspect what history, the Scriptures and other source-records offer in its support. Included in this survey will be the influences that determined the form of the doctrine and guided it to its strong place in the Church's life and thought.

3. Our third chapter will attempt a critical estimate of this doctrine of Apostolic Episcopacy, with a view especially to appraising the claim that Episcopacy is essential to the Church as ensuring for her Ministers, as no other Order can, their Apostolic basis and character. This weighing of the case for bishops as wearing the mantle of the Apostles will debouch on the question whether the data commonly adduced to warrant this understanding of Apostolic Succession are capable of an alternate construction, equally loyal to the reality of Succession, but giving it a somewhat different formulation.

4. In our fourth and final division, the principles that have emerged in our study will be put in order and an effort made to outline the Doctrine of the Ministry demanded by them. Then will follow suggestions looking to the meaning of this Doctrine for our conception of the Church, and for the issues facing the Churches in the areas instanced; that is, as the Churches seek to understand and resolve their own differences, and as together they explore the paths God is making for them through the mazes of distraction into which contemporary man has strayed.

Chapter 1

THE DOCTRINE OF APOSTOLIC EPISCOPAL SUCCESSION

THIS doctrine, as was stated in our Introduction, has a foremost place among conceptions of the Ministry, and it is a centre of eager debate whenever the subject of the Ministry is discussed. It will engage our interest in this study as providing guidance in many of the directions our thought will take, and by its forthrightness enabling us, even when our conclusions do not copy it wholly, to clarify and define them by reference to it. We shall, in this first chapter, outline the doctrine under two heads: first, its nature; second, its values to those by whom it is professed.

I

The Nature of the Doctrine of Apostolic Episcopal Succession

The *Ordinal* of the Church of England (*The Form and Manner of Making Ordaining and Consecrating of Bishops Priests and Deacons*, as in The Book of Common Prayer) opens with the words: " It is evident unto all men diligently reading Holy Scripture and Ancient Authors, that from the Apostles' time there have been these Orders of Ministers in Christ's Church: Bishops, Priests, and Deacons." This from the *Ordinal* contains the fact on which this first part of our inquiry hinges: the presence in the Church throughout her history of ministers known as 'Bishops', together with the other ministries thus named. The great classical Anglican expositor of Church Polity and the Ministry, Richard Hooker, substantiates and expands this declaration in the *Ordinal*, as he writes:

11

Out of Holy Scripture, it clearly appeareth that Churches apostolic did know but three degrees in the power of ecclesiastical order, at the first Apostles, Presbyters, and Deacons, afterwards instead of Apostles, Bishops . . . The ancientist of the Fathers mention those three degrees of ecclesiastical order specified and no more . . . There are at this day in the Church of England no other than the same degrees of ecclesiastical order, namely Bishops, Presbyters, and Deacons, which had their beginning from Christ and His blessed Apostles themselves.[1]

Neither Hooker nor the *Ordinal* claims complete or exclusive necessity for the three orders of Ministers. Hooker forcefully upholds them, particularly the rule of bishops in the Church, but as having the endorsement of Christian history and of instructed Christian understanding, rather than as laid upon the Church by divine institute or command. Episcopacy, to his mind, is the proper and essentially reasonable form of ecclesiastical order. This means that Hooker does not teach the special doctrine of Episcopacy we are bringing forward in this chapter. He has been the inspirer not of a party but of all Anglicans, of Low and Broad as well as High Church Anglican thought.

Others who were his contemporaries, however, or who came soon after, advanced this belief about Episcopacy within the Church to fuller precision in maintaining explicitly that bishops are not only in the place of the Apostles but are specially and uniquely the inheritors of the authority Christ gave to them. One who wrote in this way was John Scott (1639-95) who, as cited by Professor E. R. Fairweather, "defines the episcopal office as 'nothing else but only the apostolical superiority derived from the hands of the Apostles in a continued succession from one generation to another'."[2] A second example is John Potter, afterwards Archbishop of Canterbury, who wrote in 1707: "As our Lord was sent by God the Father to establish a Church in the world, so the Apostles were authorized by our Lord to enlarge and govern the Church after His Ascension, and

[1] *Ecclesiastical Polity*, V, lxxviii.
[2] *Episcopacy Re-Asserted*, p. 32.

they derived the same authority to their successors the Bishops."[1] These short citations give already the thread of the doctrine that is our present subject, but we add the following others for our double need of its ampler statement and of seeing how it is expressed in our own day:

The Apostles must be supposed to have had a temporary function in their capacity of founders under Christ. In this capacity they held an office by its very nature not permanent —the office of bearing the original witness to Christ's resurrection and making the original proclamation of the Gospel. But underlying this was another—a pastorate of souls, a stewardship of divine mysteries. This office, instituted in their persons, was intended to become perpetual, and that by being transmitted from its first depositaries. It was thus intended that there should be in each generation an authoritative stewardship of the grace and truth which came by Jesus Christ and a recognized power to transmit it, derived from above by apostolic descent. The men who from time to time were to hold the various offices involved in the ministry would receive their authority to minister in whatever capacity, their qualifying consecration, from above, in such sense that every ministerial act would be performed under the shelter of a commission, received by the transmission of the original pastoral authority which had been delegated by Christ Himself to His Apostles.[2]

When I consecrate a godly and well-learned man to the office and rank of Bishop in the Church of God, I do not act as the representative of the Church, if by that is meant the whole number of contemporary Christians; but I do act as the ministerial instrument of Christ in His Body the Church. The authority by which I act is His, transmitted to me through His Apostles and those to whom they committed it; I hold it neither from the Church nor apart from the Church, but from Christ in the Church.[3]

The apostolic foundation is permanent. . . If the gift of the Spirit to the Church is 'first apostles' (I Cor. 12: 28;

[1] *Discourse on Church Government,* quoted in Kirk (ed.), *The Apostolic Ministry,* p. 443.
[2] Gore, *The Church and the Ministry,* pp. 58, 59.
[3] W. Temple, *Christian Unity and Church Reunion,* pp. 18, 19.

Eph. 4: 11), it must be apostles to the end. The Church is in figure and in truth a living organism. As such it has an extensive power of self-adjustment; it can vary its organization. But there is something it cannot vary, or it will lose its identity. . . [Paul knew] that the body grows from a beginning, with continuous life, that its great functions are not interchangeable, and that there is no new beginning. When he said that the first gift of the Spirit to the Body of Christ was the Apostolate, and resolutely magnified that office, he cannot have supposed that it was to be eliminated, or that its functions were to be transferred to men of another order. The Apostolate which was first will also be last; it is permanent. . . Then where do we find it now? We answer without hesitation that it is identical with the Episcopate. I think there is no other serious claimant.[1]

If it be true that the Church is the Body of Christ, it is also true that the development of that Body through the centuries must have some bearing upon its essential nature. Its development cannot have been a haphazard development if the Church is informed by the Holy Spirit. Now it is clear that within a very short time after the initial historical impulse which gave rise to the Christian movement, that movement had articulated its ministry into such form that the episcopate had been accepted as the ordaining agent for the Church. And once it had been so articulated, it was preserved with a surprising tenacity. It would therefore seem to be in some genuine sense integral to the Church as the Body of Christ.[2]

These excerpts are lengthy, but they have done what we asked of them; they have set out sufficiently for our purpose the conception of the Ministry we are making a central issue throughout this work. The sum of this conception as they convey it is that when Christ called the Apostles and commissioned them to preach and exercise oversight in His Church, He established a Ministry which, of His will and by the guiding action of the Holy Spirit, was handed on and has continued down the years in the Order of Bishops,

[1] Lacey, *The Anglo-Catholic Faith,* p. 82.
[2] Pittenger, *His Body the Church,* pp. 80, 81.

14

and is still, in them, the Church's foundational Ministry. Other ministries have part in this original authentic Ministry in being episcopally ordained. Churches without bishops do not have in its fulness this one true Apostolic Ministry. "The Protestant Churches," writes E. R. Fairweather, "have presbyters and prophets, but no apostles."[1] Dom Gregory Dix sees Protestantism as having discarded, while Catholicism has retained, the "perpetual principle" of the Ministry. This principle again is Apostolicity preserved in the Episcopate, and it is perpetual as having been instituted by Christ ("dominically instituted") and bequeathed from "the Church order of the Apostolic age".[2] Nor is this bequest—on the Protestant side the lack—one of order or office alone. The above passages further reveal it as inward and effectual in being transmissive of those vitalities of Power *(δύναμις)* and Authority *(ἐξουσία)* which were at the first Christ's gift to His Ministers (Lk. 9: 1), and were bestowed to abide as the assurance of Him everywhere and for ever in the life of the Church (Mt. 28: 18-20; Acts 1: 8).

The foregoing paragraphs have given in fair outline the doctrine we are contemplating, but one or two directions of its meaning must be produced if we are to have its full force. A chief instance is the way this doctrine, in deriving the Ministry which Episcopacy assures to the Church from Christ's "gift of Ministry", focuses an element of deepest consequence for any view of the Ministry: the unity of the Ministry with Christ. This unity for many who profess this doctrine comes to full vision in the relation of the Ministry —as of the Church—to the Incarnation. This is a connection of the study of the Ministry that appears prominently in expositions of this doctrine, and our own brief survey must take account of it.

A question on which Protestant theology has employed itself all too little is that of the range or scope of the Incarnation. Is it identical with Jesus in His proper being as we meet Him in history? Or does it extend to other aspects of

[1] Fairweather and Hettlinger, *Episcopacy and Reunion*, p. 24.
[2] In Kirk (ed.), *op. cit.*, p. 303.

that total Event or Epoch of which He is the centre and determining power?

The following will set this issue in its place in our study:

> If the form of the Church is conditioned by the circumstances under which God chose to become incarnate, then the " scandal of particularity " which faces us in the Son of God who came as Israel's Messiah confronts us also in the Church, His Body. Unless we are prepared to deny the finality of the revelation in Christ for Christian faith, we must admit that it makes a real difference to Christianity in every age that God willed to be born of blessed Mary, and to live among His ancient people as the human individual, Jesus of Nazareth. One of the forms, however, which this difference takes, is to be seen in the worship and order of the Church, whose characteristic pattern owes its origin to the fact that God's ancient people was *this* people, the old Israel. . . The enduring significance, then, of the Christianized elements of Jewish custom, from which the essential structure of the Catholic order developed, must be appreciated, if the full implications of the Incarnation itself are to be understood.[1]

What this tells us is not simply that the ways of the people among whom Jesus came had part in shaping the movement that arose from Him—this is generally owned, and is of the nature of historical happening; but that these same circumstances were woven into the character of the movement, to become for all future historical Christianity a part of the reality of it. This is true *a fortiori* of those elements of the background whence grew the Catholic forms of Church worship and order. To adhere to Church and Ministry as they then came into being is to possess the modes of these which the Incarnation, occurring when and where it did, formed unto itself, and which in consequence are not its vehicle only but derive from it and share its essential quality.

This essential affinity of Church and Ministry and the Incarnation has been the theme of impressive testimony and

[1] Fairweather, in Fairweather and Hettlinger, *op. cit.*, pp. 10, 11.

16

acclaim. It will assist our purpose to note one or two examples.

First, as to the Church.

The following from within Greek Orthodoxy:

> What is the Church? . . . Few stop to consider the "on-tology" of the Church, that to which the creed refers in the phrase, "I believe . . . the Church!" Though it has its empirically visible embodiment, yet the Church itself is out-side the scope of our empirical mode of knowledge; it is, in fact, matter of faith . . . The Church is more than an institu-tion which happened to appear in history . . . the Church transcends history, and belongs not to time alone, but to eternity. It is not merely that it is of divine institution, its mode of existence is divine; and its existence in God is prior to, antecedes and conditions its historical existence. . . . The Church is properly uncreated and yet it enters into the history of mankind. That implies that it has a theandric character; it is, in fact, God-manhood *in actu*. . . . In so far as it is grounded in God, the Church is divine Wisdom. Equally in its earthly historical existence, it is created Wis-dom. In the Church the two aspects of Wisdom are entirely, inseparably and unconfusedly united. . . . The definition at Chalcedon of the mode of union of the two natures in Christ was at bottom a definition of the Church.[1]

From Roman Catholic sources:

> The Church itself is part of the revealed reality. . . . The Church, as the Body of Christ, is itself one of the mysteries of faith. . . . She is the Body of Christ . . . because Christ has formed a Body to Himself . . . The Church possesses a super-natural character in this sense that, notwithstanding her being a human society, she is not determined as to her essence and her essential manifestations by the character of the human beings who compose her, but exclusively by Christ and the Holy Spirit.[2]

Our faith should never make separate what God has joined together: *sacramentum magnum in Christo et in*

[1] Bulgakov, *The Wisdom of God*, pp. 199, 201.
[2] van de Pol, *The Christian Dilemma: Catholic Church—Reformation*, pp. 77, 78, 159.

ecclesia. If Christ is the sacrament of God, the Church is for us the sacrament of Christ; she represents Him in the full and ancient meaning of the term, she really makes Him present. . . . Jesus, our Saviour, took the elements of His body from our race. . . . In like manner His Church; it is humanity that provides it with a body. . . . In her, man's desires and God's have their meeting-place . . . Like its Founder it is eternal and sure of itself . . . The Church is at home everywhere, and everyone should feel himself at home in the Church. Thus the risen Christ takes on the countenance of all races and each hears Him in his own tongue.[1]

One further comment on the Church, from a Presbyterian teacher, will reveal that these high beliefs about the Church professed by the older Churches are not, as to some of their principles, an offence to Evangelical Protestants:

The Church is a part of the fact of Christ. . . . Christ is not merely an individual man . . . His is a uniquely inclusive Personality . . . We are now able to discern what the Church is in its creative and constitutive principles, prior to any expression of them in historical form. It is far more and other than a human association . . . It is more even than an apostolic or divine institution . . . It is, in its essence, a fact about Christ Himself—the fact, namely, that, uniting men in vital relationship with Himself, He unites them in fellowship with one another in Him. This is the Church which is not merely descended from Christ . . . but is '*in* God the Father and *in* the Lord Jesus Christ'! This is the Church which is really a part of what Jesus Christ was and is. This is the Church which, therefore, rightly is named in the Creed among the spiritual facts of faith . . . Not only deeper than any expression in history but also prior to it, in the region of faith, are this union and communion in Christ.[2]

We can read beneath their words deep differences among these several writers, but they leave this as common to them: the Church is more than the company or brotherhood of those who have joined themselves to Jesus; it is

[1] Lubac, *Catholicism: A Study of Dogma in Relation to the Corporate Destiny of Mankind*, pp. 28, 29, 147, 153, 154.
[2] Carnegie Simpson, *Church Principles*, pp. 17, 18, 21, 22.

more even than is conveyed in speaking (as is frequent today) of the Church as the continuation of the Incarnation, if the thought simply is of the Church as carrying or extending the Incarnation into subsequent history through her own historical existence and mission. As well as being in temporal continuity with the Incarnation, the Church is in these four texts incorporate within it. The Church *continues* the Incarnation by her nature as being *of* it. Bulgakov soars to the ontological plane to say of the Church what ordinarily we say of Christ; it, as He, is preëxistent and uncreate. Lubac and van de Pol move the same way; though neither they nor Simpson would minimize, for something in the realm of transcendence, the reality of the Church in the world. As to *this* Church, in the matter we turned to their words to illustrate the four are at one; they would all claim that the Church as it appeared in history had its own place as a moment of the καιρός or divine ingress into our world whence Christianity arose. There is no ground for a Christianity without the Church, since God's sovereign gift to men in the coming of Christ embraced, equally with all else comprehended by it, the gift of fellowship (κοινωνία) to those who received Him. Pittenger, perhaps, if we may add a fifth to the above four, has put this position in boldest form. "The Incarnation of God in Christ," he writes, "caused there to come into being a society which was knit to that Christ . . . The supreme and crucial act of God for men is not Christ alone, nor is it Christ and His Church; rather it is Christ-Church . . . The Church as the unity whose informing life is the very life of the divine-human Lord, is as much part of the Gospel as that Lord Himself . . . as much part of the faith of the Christian." It is this living unity of the Church with Christ that enables her "to continue the incarnating activity."[1] Not all who on the whole share Pittenger's outlook would endorse fully his language as here shown; but his words make vivid the principle they and he together do hold: the Church of its nature and origin an essential participant in God's self-bestowal and purpose in His gift of Jesus Christ.

[1] *op. cit.*, pp. 6, 7, 90.

This in regard to the Church. But our interest centres more closely and directly in the Ministry. Is anything comparable on record concerning it?

In answer, we recall to the reader the passage from Fairweather on the Incarnation and Catholic Order, as on a previous page.[1] Other similar references are these:

From the bishops assembled at Lambeth:

> We believe that in those principles of the Church's life we have inherited, with their historic continuity in the spheres alike of Faith and Order, we have at once a treasure and a source of stability which are of special worth in an age when all traditions and conventions are called in question . . . In the experience of many of us this heritage of Faith and Order seems to be one and indivisible, and to have its roots in the redemptive method of God in the Incarnation.[2]

From Bishop Gore:

> The ministry corresponds in principle to the Incarnation and the sacraments, and, indeed, to the original creation of man. In all these cases the material comes from below. " Of the dust of the ground the Lord God formed man." Christ's humanity is of real physical origin of the stock of Adam. The material of the sacraments is common water, " bread of the earth ", common wine. But this material, which is of the earth, is in each case assumed (though not in each case in the same sense) by the Spirit from above. " God breathed into man's nostrils the breath of life." The Divine Son assumes the humanity and makes it redemptive. A consecration from above comes upon the sacrament; " the bread which is of the earth ", which man offers for the divine acceptance, " receiving the invocation of God, is no longer common bread, but Eucharist, made up of two things, an earthly and a heavenly ".[3] In each of these cases we have the material offered from below and the empowering consecration from above. It is just these two elements that are present to con-

---

[1] *supra*, p. 16.
[2] *The Lambeth Conference, 1930*, p. 119.
[3] Irenaeus, *Adversus Haereses*, IV, xviii, 5.

stitute the ministry. Those who are to be ordained are . . . the offering of the people; but they receive their consecration from above . . . It would appear that Christ founded not only a Church but an apostolate in the Church . . . this apostolic office included all that was necessary to perpetuate that mission on which the Father had sent the Son into the world.[1]

The Ministry, then, even as the Church, can be interlinked with the Incarnation; this is done in these several writings, again not in identical ways if we compare them strictly, yet to this measure of identity: the Ministry of its nature conforms to that total and plenteous divine offering wherein God made overture to His world and opened the way of its return to Him. Christ, Church, Sacraments and Ministry are one unity, of one divine-human structure of being; the Incarnation, " the sacrament of our salvation " in Tertullian's phrase, compasses and is the paradigm of them all. The Ministry is of the divine Gift as surely as the others; and it is not to be thought that any more than the others— Church or Sacrament—it was given to be withdrawn. It remains and must continually remain the same Ministry as at the first, as the Church is the same Church. This is the Apostolic Ministry, beginning from the Apostles in whom Christ founded this order of Ministry.

So much would be said by some who do not hold the precise view of the Ministry we are examining. Many theories of the Ministry make Christ its author and its course continuous in the Church from apostolic times. What the holders of this particular belief add as their distinctive claim is that this Apostolic Ministry, thus arising in Christ's own appointment, has from an early time had this continuance and unbroken sequence in the Episcopal Ministry. Hence it is this Ministry, the Episcopate hewn of this rock, born of God's act in sending forth His Son, that is still the Church's basal and ' essential ' Ministry.[2]

This then is the view of the Ministry, the ampler understanding of Apostolic Episcopal Succession, that results from relating Church and Ministry to the Incarnation. Episco-

---

[1] *op. cit.*, pp. 61, 62, 208, 209.　　[2] Kirk, *op. cit.*, pp. 7ff.

pacy is seen as of the Ministry that was given with the Church to abide while the Church abides; while the Succession of the Ministry becomes more than a thread of history and acquires inherent validation from the truth of the Incarnation through the fact that when the latter is conceived according to its whole nature and full historical incidence, the Ministry falls within the circuit of it as a kindred sharer of its character and aim.

The argument that leads to this result is impressive and not to be denied its force. If God truly, in Christ, came into history, then He united Himself with it at the point where He came; His presence in the world must wear the stamp of a particular history. Otherwise His coming would be a phantom that could occur anywhere, a theophany rather than a real Incarnation. Similarly the Christian movement as it sprang from Christ: it too, interacting with the social and historical *milieu*, must have been in part shaped by it. This necessity in the historical accompaniment of what God did involves that He willed the accompaniment or at least consented to it. It is a fair application of this when, as in the reference earlier,[1] "elements of Jewish custom" from the time of the Incarnation that entered into the making of Catholic order are accounted a divinely-intended constituent of that order—again from the premiss that God, not in semblance but actually, domiciled Himself in history. Such then the argument for the position of the preceding paragraph, and it points again to this conclusion: the Ministry —as the Church—grounded in the Incarnation, and its identity and character arising from this fact of such divine ordering as implies their maintenance through a Succession of Ministry. The picture is of both Church and Ministry as continuing and being permanently authentic in the manner in which they historically emerged.

It is no answer to this that this Ministry came at the first, and has ever been, loaded with temporal infirmities. Ministers are often poor vessels; bishops in the apostolic line are known to the Church's annals whose purposes and deeds were far from apostolic. There is no excusing of unnecessary

[1] *supra*, p. 16.

fault; but human and earthly limitation is no *essential* dero-
gation in Ministry or Church, as it was not in the Incarnate
Word Himself. We have all the treasures in earthen vessels.
To claim divine qualities for Church and Ministry—ye are
a royal priesthood, a holy nation (I Peter 2: 9)—in face of
the very human showing of many Churches and Ministers,
is no more 'scandalous' than beholding divine reality and
glory in a human life (John 1: 14) was to the 'wise' among
Jews and Greeks, and is still to the sophists whether of East
or West.

Let God work His own way and anoint whom He will.
The Ministry is not less under His seal through sharing the
'foolishness' of the Incarnation, the Cross and the Resurrection (I Cor. 1: 21, 23); rather is this its consecration with
them, the fulness of Ministry; it asks nothing higher. The
Incarnation has sanctified historical particularity and even
contingency, not only for itself, but for all that hangs upon
it; for the contemporary forms that gave their fashion to
Church and Ministry as arising when and where they did;
for Church and Ministry themselves, in their weakness even
as they come from Christ's own hands, in their chequered
pilgrimage from His time to ours. Frail and often faithless,
they are of Him and of His being amongst men; and it is
their unity with Him, first in the Apostles, then in those
who in their train have fulfilled their office, that gives to
them their special and holy character; gives to the Ministry
especially that highest enduement which is the true 'Gift of
Ministry', bestowed first—bestowed to be retained and
transmitted—when Christ breathed upon His first Ministers and gave the Spirit to them (John 20: 22). It is
the divinely singular 'Gift' for the Ministry's singular
task.

Our endeavour in what we have so far written has been
to outline and state the principle of the particular doctrine
of the Ministry that has given the title to this first chapter.
This doctrine avers not only that the Church possesses a
Ministry derived from Christ through the Apostles, but that
it has this Ministry by Christ's design: in the words of
Bishop Gore, "Christ founded not only a Church but an

apostolate in the Church."[1] The doctrine also is precise and positive in identifying this Ministry among the Church's Orders, naming it as one with the historic line of bishops and those who have their ministry and authority through them. We shall next proceed beyond the form to certain values of this doctrine, by virtue of which it is to many who hold it no matter of theory, but momentous and precious truth.

II

Values of the Doctrine of Apostolic Episcopal Succession

The values we shall consider are of the spiritual order. The idea that grace is imparted tactually as the bishop lays hands on those who succeed him in the episcopal office, or on those he ordains to the lesser ministerial orders, is no necessary part of belief in Apostolic Succession. "We value the Succession," wrote the Bishop of Manchester in the *Methodist Recorder* of Jan. 26, 1956, "not because we think there is a mechanical transmission of grace, but as a personal link with the remote past and indeed with the apostolic age." Through this "personal link" the Ministry continually receives fresh spiritual accessions as a direct legacy from the Apostles and Christ. This spiritual benefit is the real defence and sanction of Apostolic Episcopal Succession. We have already had hints of it; for example, in words recorded from Archbishop William Temple: "When I consecrate a godly and well-learned man to the office of bishop . . . I act as the ministerial instrument of Christ . . . The authority by which I act is His, transmitted to me through His Apostles."[2] This, however, may still seem the more formal side of the legacy; its spiritual quality will then be more apparent in the following from Archbishop Frederick Temple:

> Christ sent forth His Apostles; the Apostles received their commission from Him; they were not the organs of the congregation; they were the ministers of the Lord Himself . . . It

[1] *supra*, p. 21.   [2] *supra*, p. 13.

is for this that we insist upon the succession of the Ministry
. . . The purpose of the succession is to link the Church of
the present generation back, by steps that cannot be mis-
taken, to the first appointment of the Apostles by our Lord;
and to make men feel the unity of the Body as it comes down
the stream of history, and if possible to touch their hearts
with some sense of that Power which the Lord bequeathed
when He ascended on high and gave gifts to men.[1]

Who would withhold from any a doctrine that has this
richness for them? Apostolic Succession to those who receive
and cherish it is plainly a reality of deep and vital import;
it is not asserted—or it need not be—from pride or from
desire for prerogative; it has holier warrant. Some who do
not accept it wholly are conscious of its appeal and become
wistful. P. T. Forsyth, after describing the decline of the
Church from being the κοινωνία of those who are bound in
sacrificial loyalty to Christ to being a religio-social club,
proceeds thus:

> This is a descent that constantly troubles the more
> thorough and earnest minds among us. Some of our critics
> put it down to the lack of an episcopate or an apostolic suc-
> cession. . . . Our critics are right in so far as they mean that
> the chief necessity is a more clear, arresting, guiding and
> commanding theory of the Church and its Ministry.[2]

"A clear, arresting, guiding and commanding theory"—
so a great nonconformist theologian phrases what he deems
necessary and longs for in our thought of the Ministry, and
whose presence in the doctrine of Apostolic Succession, as
we are here thinking of it, he implicitly acknowledges;
though his own theological outlook might dictate other
expression of it. He longs for this theory for the Church's
spiritual recovery, that she might repent of her lapses and
again truly be Christ's Church.

This spiritual force of Apostolic Succession was enhanced
for Anglicans through the circumstances of their history.

[1] *Twelve Sermons preached in Truro Cathedral*, pp. 17, 21.
[2] *Lectures on the Church and Sacraments*, p. 27.

The doctrine of Succession is not a mere dogma Anglicans have inherited and still profess without knowing why. There was much fluidity of belief in the classical age of Anglicanism; even Hooker, as seen already, firmly espousing Episcopacy, pauses short of claiming full necessity for it. One could almost say that generally for Tudor and post-Tudor Anglicans Episcopacy was of the *bene esse* of the Church rather than the *esse*. The Stuart divines were more concerned about " No Bishop, no King" than about " No Bishop, no Church." Nevertheless, the course of the Reformation in England led to the riper doctrine, though in part through reversion from certain of its developments as well as by its direct trend. Anglicans had to meet those who claimed divine authority for Presbytery; the crystallizing of their ecclesiological faith about Episcopacy enshrined a not unnatural counter-claim. But there was a deeper movement in the Anglican spirit that engendered a positive advance. It grew from the way the Supremacy of Henry VIII and the Settlement under Elizabeth faced the Church with the problem of Church and State. Earnest Anglicans have always been alert to this problem. It is a mistake to think that Anglicans in Britain take glory from being the Established Church and by reason of it are at one in looking upon Nonconformity from superior heights. Many of them would willingly be rid of the Establishment; many more have been alive to its drawbacks and dangers. In the Life and Liberty Movement, carried on by groups in the Church of England between the two world wars, the leaders, a chief of whom was William Temple, declared plainly: " If the Church is to have new life, it must have liberty . . . the power to control its own life, even at the cost, if necessary, of disestablishment."[1]

This tension with the State has wrought powerfully to turn the Church's mind to its own being and to re-enliven its zeal for its Episcopal Ministry standing secure and stable on its divine foundation. The men who have felt most straitened under the Establishment are precisely those who have gained greatest strength and reassurance from Apostolic

[1] Iremonger, *William Temple: Life and Letters*, p. 227.

26

Episcopal Succession. It has been a buttress against Erastian subserviency and has fortified the liberty of prophesying to have, besides and beyond Crown and Government, an allegiance direct to God and Christ through a Ministry of the very order Christ Himself gave. The monumental proof of all this was the Tractarian movement of the mid-nineteenth century which, again from the spiritual impulsion and interest, gave still further momentum to belief in Apostolic Succession and confirmed many Churchmen in it. At the beginning of this movement Keble, in his sermon on *National Apostasy*, claimed respect for the Church not as a national institution but as an Instrument of the Divine Will, and denounced as "grievous sin" political interference with the pastoral authority of the bishops, "the successors of the Apostles." The Tractarian leaders, writes Wilfred L. Knox,

> proclaiming the sacramental system of the Catholic Church as the divinely appointed means by which man has access to God, insisted that the Church was not a department of the State for the preservation of sound morality on a vaguely religious basis, but the living representative of God on earth appointed to preserve and proclaim the truth revealed by Jesus Christ and inspired by the abiding presence of the Holy Spirit.[1]

This ideal of the Church and the awakened zeal for the ministry of the Episcopate as sacramental and apostolic have gone hand in hand within this Catholic revival in the Church of England; and their joint service has been immense toward continued purifying of the Church from political servility and in girding her independence. Apostolic Episcopal Succession, then, as we have seen it in these paragraphs, has been in several periods and phases of the Church a pillar of freedom and the nurturer and support of spirituality in charging and constraining the Church's devotion, not to her temporal head or worldly station, but to her One Supreme Head, the Divine Saviour Himself. Divine

[1] *The Catholic Movement in the Church of England*, pp. 213, 214.

instrumentality within the Church and direction of her life, as against State or any secular ordering, is for many the purport of this doctrine.

It may be thought that, proper as all this may seem under English skies, it has little general relevancy. Apostolic Succession as a spiritual counterpoise to undue State infringement may yield much in lands where the Church is "by law established," but loses its interest where Churches are autonomous communions. In Canada we have no established Church and in religion face no threat of direct civil domination. But there is a social Erastianism, perhaps more deadly than the other which is political or national. There are vested powers, sociological and cultural conditionings and pressures, that can deflect the Church as effectually as legal compulsion can do, from her essence and true vocation.

> The danger which confronts any Church in a settled society is that it inclines to fall back into paganism which sanctifies uncritically the natural seasons and the natural institutions. . . . Religious institutions are constantly tempted to plan their strategy in terms of a pattern which is sufficiently set to be visible and not in terms of a situation whose direction it is possible to change.[1]

Or more expressly from Forsyth:

> A Church may be established in practice, when it is not in law. . . . A Church may be on quite happy terms with the world; and its Christ may be made welcome because He is "so human" . . . Thus a Church becomes established by the world when it is not by the State. . . . There is hardly a Church that has not suffered from its success . . . suffered in its power of witnessing the Gospel . . . while this is true fatally of the dynastic Churches, it is also in its measure true of some Churches of the democracy which stand aloof from politics much more than from Mammon. To be rid of politics is not to be free from the world.[2]

[1] Jenkins, *Tradition, Freedom, and the Spirit*, pp. 173, 174.
[2] *op. cit.*, pp. 7, 8, 65, 66.

These are frank words and they mean: whatever the Church's social setting, whether that of State Church or of 'Free' Churches so named in distinction from it, the Church always meets the world and in the presence of its hostilities and even more its flatteries needs to keep ever-vigilant guard of her liberty in the Gospel and her prophetic calling. What then so likely to afford this guard or hold the Church to this calling as a Ministry unfettered to all worldly orders in being divinely formed and enabled? Succession from the Apostles, so the confidence of those whose belief we are reviewing, goes far to assure this Ministry. For Ministry so arising is plainly not of human fashioning, coming as it does from the Church's Divine Lord who chose the Apostles and gave His authority to them, and of whose similar choice men ever since have been named to like place and task. Here is Ministry for the Church of such divine ordainment as sets and furbishes it to admonish and judge the powers of the age, not to succumb to them. Can the Church forgo this Ministry or have Ministry of any other origin, and challenge the time? The answer comes in words given in our Introduction: "The Church can go forward conquering and to conquer, only as an instrument divinely forged, and as she can claim that her Ministry derives direct from the Lord Himself."[1] It is Ministry from Christ through the Apostles that can be held to be so derived.

These meanings of Apostolic Episcopal Succession should be understood by those who do not hold the doctrine, and should be included in any estimation of the attitude of those who not only hold it but gain succour and compulsion from it. These believers in the doctrine sometimes seem assertive and exclusive, claiming for Ministers of their own Communions what they do not grant to those of others. But they are not assertive of will or from perverseness; their claims have their fibre from earnest conviction. They revere the Historic Episcopate as having its form from the foundations, as "going beyond the perversions of history to the original conception of the Apostolic Ministry."[2] Their persuasion of

---

[1] Kirk, *vide supra*, p. 9.   [2] *The Lambeth Conference, 1920*, p. 115.

this has a formative place in their Christian outlook and answers their concern for the integrity and purity of the Gospel as descended from Apostolic hands.

This is a concern, however, that belongs to all Christians; the values of Apostolic Succession that bind so many Christians to it are as values proper to them all. Difference enters when certain forms in Ministry and Ordinance are made the chief or even the one vehicle of these values. May there not, it can be asked, be various vehicles, severally appropriate to time and place or to religious predilection and habitude? Is not Christianity of the spirit, and the unity Christians should seek a unity of life, let forms and other externals fall as they may?

In reply we are reminded that the Church in the New Testament is the *Body* of Christ, and it is consonant to this figure for the Church that she have corporate being and unity as well as—and as expressing—unity of spirit. Did not Christ so will for His followers, calling them not alone to some inner, invisible accord, but to be a people, seen and known as such by the world (John 13: 35)? Then further in this reply the charge is laid that under the doctrine of the Church as spiritual, as the invisible Church "known to God only," the true Church is *dis*embodied and ministries and ordinances being of the Body are removed from the Church's true or essential order to the accessory and relative. They can then appropriately show the variability natural to the relative. But by the conception this reply is defending, which attributes the Church's visible and corporeal being equally with her transcendence and hiddenness to the divine intention, the Ministry even as to its form is of one nature with the Church and rightfully shares its permanency. If the Church as corporeal is divinely willed, a divine provision must be assumed in what sustains it and gives its order to it. Orders of Ministry have this relation and function; they are organs of the Body for its unity and upbuilding (Eph. 4: 11-13).

Hence the Church's care is not just with the values the Ministry subserves, but with the Ministry as their divinely-elected Instrument; the characters that pertain to them

extend to it. The values are the maintenance and furtherance of the Church's spiritual and corporate life and her
common testimony. The complement to this is a common
and continuing Ministry divinely certified for it. Where,
then, is this Ministry? The consensus of history, it is held,
reveals it in the Episcopal Ministry.

> If the Church was from the first intended to be outwardly
> one, the cardinal point of this outward unity lies in the
> appointment and recognition of its official authorities. In
> fact, from the second century onwards the duly appointed
> bishops of sees were looked upon as the organs and guardians
> of the unity of the Church. . . . Recognized validity of Orders
> in bishops and priests was the link whereby the body of the
> Church was held together.[1]

By this account, the doctrine of the Ministry before us in
this chapter only transcribes the *fact* of Ministry as God
gave it and as the Church through most of her history has
possessed it. It is Ministry or Orders of Ministers not adjec-
tival to the Church whose being can be thought apart from
them, but with Faith and the Word an integral sharer in
that being. It is not that the *given* of Christianity is Faith
which assumes or makes to itself Order for its action and
realization in history; Faith and Order are historically
coeval, "twin pillars of Catholicism" this same writer
names them.[2] This is a note we have met before, in the
Lambeth declaration regarding the Church's "heritage of
Faith and Order as one and indivisible,"[3] and it expresses a
position in which we may well see the peak of our outline
of Apostolic Episcopacy; though the following third
example of the position from Dr. Leonard Hodgson may
make this more apparent:

> For the Anglican, unity means unity vertically down the
> ages as well as horizontally across the face of the earth. . . . He
> notices that in any earthly society unity and continuity from
> generation to generation seem to depend on two factors inter-

[1] Quick, *The Christian Sacraments*, p. 140.
[2] *ibid.*, p. 153.   [3] *supra*, p. 20.

woven like two strands of a single rope: the outward continuity of organization and the inward continuity of spirit,
faith and practice. . . . He notices, for example, that if any
body of trustees are challenged as to their right to continue
administering some endowment, they have to make good
their position by showing that they have been appointed con-
stitutionally in accordance with the accepted custom of the
trust, and that in their administering they are carrying out
the intentions of the founder as he would like them to be
carried out were he alive at the time. He concludes that he
cannot rightly exercise less care in matters spiritual than is
required in matters temporal, that he cannot offer to baptize
into the fellowship of the Apostles if he is careless about
either strand of the rope which links the Church of today to
the Church of the Upper Room.[1]

This is a great conception, this twofold unity of the
Church through space and time. It brings a rebuke to
Churches whose approach to unity is cross-sectional or uni-
lateral. In what it says of the time or 'vertical' aspect, this
passage from Dr. Hodgson gives still another instance of
what we saw earlier to be a deep stratum of the doctrine of
Apostolic Ministry, the fount of Ministry in God's purpose
in the Incarnation and in the Faith's historical beginnings.
But we bring these words in at this place for their other
phase. In common with the two other references they lead
to what we say is the peak of the belief we are studying:
the principle that the Church is of divine appointment both
in her Faith and Order, so that the factors that form the
Order and the elements of Faith are alike of her abiding
being; they are 'strands' of one thread. The context of the
references makes clear that woven inseparably into the
'strand' of Order is the Ministry the Episcopate has served
to keep one and unsevered since Apostolic times. Apostolic
Episcopal Succession becomes by this showing *co-ordinate
in the Church's life with the progress of the Faith itself.*

This is a result to satisfy its most ardent advocates, hence
fittingly the culminating word of our positive discourse
upon it. Save that we may add as of interest that Dr. Hodg-

[1] *Essays in Christian Philosophy*, p. 144.

son sees his principles being proved in contacts that are occurring between the Church of England and other Churches. In a further writing, he recalls from his former work the paragraph we have inserted from him, and adds: " The action taken by the Church of England in its negotiations with the Churches of Finland, Latvia and Esthonia illustrates this attitude, and shows that on the side of outward organization the apostolic succession is regarded as one of those valuable elements of the Catholic tradition which we treasure for ourselves and wish to share with others."[1] These words if we had nothing more would warrant our present section on the *value* to the Church's work and life of Apostolic Succession in the experience of those who are devoutly persuaded of it.

We shall now give a summary of what we have attempted in this chapter, setting it in line with the view held of the importance of the Ministry in general Catholic teaching.

The doctrine of Apostolic Episcopal Succession rests on the belief that, in providing salvation for men, God also provided the means by which the salvation might reach men, this means being in the form of certain institutes and acts through which the divine saving energy becomes accessible to those by whom it is sought. These institutes are the Church and her ordinances, especially the sacraments, and her authorized and authentic Ministry. "The Catholic Churches understand themselves as the concrete channels through which God's revelation in Jesus is spread into the lives of men."[2] Or as one writes from within the Catholic household: "Communion between God and the soul may take the form of prayer, or it may take the form of some external action to the proper performance of which a special promise of grace is attached. The latter form of communion with God is the sacramental system of the Catholic Church."[3] The Ministry belongs to this Order for mediating God's grace and saving presence as truly as the other

---

[1] *Intercommunion (supra, p. 8), pp. 260, 261.
[2] Pauck, *The Heritage of the Reformation*, p. 139.
[3] W. L. Knox, *op. cit.*, p. 51.

C

constituents of it. " A Church to be Catholic must hold the Catholic Faith, treasure the Catholic Scriptures, administer the Catholic Sacraments, and retain the Catholic Ministry."[1] To this Ministry it belongs to make known the Word of salvation, to guard this Word from perversion and corruption, to celebrate the sacramental ordinances, to help and guide men in their search for the salvation, and to instruct and counsel them when, having embraced it, they desire fuller realization and certainty of it.

This Ministry, with these necessary tasks and offices, began when Christ named the Apostles; it has continued through history in Orders of Ministers emanating from them. Hence it is of the dispensation of Christianity; with the Gospel and the Church, of the Foundation divinely laid, of the one Christianity built on the Foundation. It remains perpetually to the Church, even as her Faith and Word remain; with them to be received as given, not shaped to our will; to be adapted to need and exigence but consistently with maintaining its appointed order. Catholics of whatever branch so receive the Ministry; they cherish it as upholding the spiritual estate of the Church and the authority of her Word as not of men. Not lowest in the Church's regard is the way this Ministry signalizes and has in substantial part secured the unity and continuity of Christian Faith and Order in all ages and lands.

To those who find an incongruity in annexing external or visible media to a Gift of Salvation in its essence spiritual, Catholics have a ready answer. The conjunction is valid *prima facie* in a world such as ours. Divine powers reaching down to our temporal and material life must move into its channels and employ its instrumentalities; as is the witness again of the Incarnation wherein the divine Word drew closest to historical man in the ' fashion ' and through the agencies of the historical. How then in turn could the Gospel of divine salvation have become effectual for men without some method for promulgating it and ministering its benefits engendered from and suited to the human condition? And would not this method, so essential to

[1] Garbett, *The Claims of the Church of England*, p. 17.

Christianity's purpose, have been authorized from the first, to be the given and abiding possession of the Church? Salvation from God, in other words, has its fit replica in an institute of salvation wherein God has provided objectively for the bestowal of it. This objectivity is not mechanical but of the spirit, since in Christianity, conformably to its divine-human substance and origin, spirit is interpreted only through a correlation of objective events of salvation and subjective-personal appropriation.

Catholics charge that Protestantism destroyed this objectivity or objective salvation-order. The Reformation placed the Scriptures in the individual's own hands, and taught him to find there the mediation and the reality of God's saving grace. He could make his own personal response to the Word there encountered. This response, personal acceptance of salvation and commitment to God, became all-determining to the undermining of Catholic notions of sacramental efficacy and priestly authority. Catholics for their part do not discount personal faith and experience; but their concern is for the wholeness of Christian life which, connoting both inward and outward, has its security in such connection of them as ensures for the one, the inward, that it be established and continually renewed from the other. They see these tendencies of Protestantism as the emptying of Christianity of its communal sources of life and power, to yield their place to individual conscience and subjective spirituality. Spirituality can be a greater danger to Christianity than materialism when it forgets that if Christianity is a common redemption it must have its vitality and truth from its objective-historical subsistence, not solely in spiritual states. Make it dominantly a religious consciousness and the door is open for personal religious caprice to obliterate its world-meaning. Catholics, as we say, not disowning the personal and experimental, put their premium on the communal and objective and lean for its sustenance on the forms which they maintain were given for that end with Christianity itself.

Apostolic Episcopal Succession turns strongly the Catholic way in these Catholic-Protestant divergences. For it too regards Christianity as *Common Life in the Body of Christ*[1] as well as private religious emotion; and it believes as surely that the foundational and other structures first divinely set within the *Body* for its upbuilding ought to continue of it to the end of the Church's temporal phase. One doesn't build a house and then proceed repeatedly to alter its basic and structural plan while still intending it to be the same house. Similarly, for the Body of Christ in the world to continue the one Body identifiable as itself, the institutions that were originally wrought into its fabric must be accounted, in F. D. Maurice's phrase, "themselves living portions of it."[2] Pre-eminent among the institutes the Church thus had from the beginning was the Ministry of the Apostles; can the Church then truly be the Church without this Ministry? Apostolic Succession gives answer affirming the need for this Ministry and adding the claim that the Church possesses it in the Episcopal Ministry whose spiritual pedigree reaches back to the Apostles; and it is this Episcopal Ministry the Church should maintain for the very reason that it means for her existence and identity what the Apostolate meant through the extension to it, and the exercise by it down the descent from the Apostles, of the authority—the commission and charge—the Apostles themselves received.

There are, as was seen earlier, degrees in the avowal of this claim. It is a mistake to think of Apostolic Succession in the form in which we have considered it as the doctrine of the Anglican Church as such, however influential in this and other Churches are the groups that profess it. To many Churchmen, Episcopacy is the Church's 'regular' rather than 'essential' Ministry, necessary for the fulness of the Church, uniquely vital to her wellbeing (*bene esse*), but not strictly of the *esse*. Others go farther: "the episcopate," writes one of them, "is the only means by which our Lord's commission to stand in His Person before God and man is given afresh to each new minister of His Church."[3] In our

---

[1] Title of a book by Father Thornton.
[2] *The Kingdom of Christ*, ii, 525.
[3] Gregory Dix, in *The Apostolic Ministry*, p. 303.

outline of the doctrine we have not been unmindful of what is common to those who affirm it, though placing in the foreground, for the reasons given at the opening of this chapter, its more thoroughgoing expression. We have dwelt too on the earnestness with which the doctrine is upheld, and the spiritual vitalities that are felt to belong to it and that help to explain its firm ascendancy over wide areas of the Church. There is the further question whether these vitalities and values, rightfully put in association with this view of the Ministry, depend solely upon it, or could co-subsist with other, in important ways different, conceptions of the Ministry. Our sequel will have here a principal issue.

Meanwhile we turn, in the next chapter, to the facts pertaining to the Ministry in its first institution and in its development in the formative period of the Church. Our purpose in this will be to bring to view the Scriptural, historical and other data whence the principle of Apostolic Succession is derived and which are most widely cited in its support.

Chapter 2

Our inquiry takes us now to the New Testament, to what Jesus said and did as it belongs to our study of the beginning of the Ministry, and to tendencies with respect to the Ministry in the primitive and apostolic Church. From this we shall proceed one further stage, beyond the age of the Apostles, to include in our survey the crystallization of forms of Ministry in the pre-Nicene centuries. We shall search in all these phases for what is pertinent to and has been or can be counted to favour the doctrine of the Apostolic-Episcopal Ministry.

I

What Jesus did toward the Creation of the Ministry

I may begin by confessing to an initial murmur of protest when anyone speaks of Jesus as *instituting* a Ministry, or even as *giving* a Ministry to His Church. It goes contrary to what I have felt about Jesus, to picture Him as acting in so formal and precise a way. Jesus goes here and there, teaching and healing. He ministers to this one, then to another, but leaves no one behind Him to foster the impression or organize any who have shown interest. He talks long with the woman at the well, but doesn't return the next day to follow up a promising beginning. He doesn't tabulate successes or keep names on a list. He can leave the sequel and outcome of His work to the Word as He speaks it and men hear and to the Spirit who as need calls will guide the movement He has inaugurated and raise up human instruments and helpers. Jesus Himself giving forms to this movement, instituting orders and ordinances to have permanent place within it—*instituting* anything as we commonly understand the word—does not tally with the sort of being which, as I read the Gospels, I feel Him to be.

Schweitzer adds fuel to this feeling in this well-known passage:

> He comes to us as One unknown, without a name, as of old, by the lakeside, He came to those who knew Him not. He speaks to us the same word: "Follow thou Me," and sets us to the tasks which He has to fulfil for our time. He commands. And to those who obey Him, whether they be wise or simple, He will reveal Himself in the toils, the conflicts, the sufferings which they shall pass through in His fellowship, and as an ineffable mystery, they shall learn in their own experience who He is.[1]

If this is the real Jesus, then He—this unknown and nameless One, coming, calling, then leaving us to discover by obeying—seems as remote as can be from the organizer with his pre-thought plans. Not that this forbids organization to His followers: forms and systems, though not authorized by Him expressly, may be legitimate if they are consonant with His spirit; or necessary if, in the circumstances of the given time, they are the appropriate vehicle for transmitting His purpose and influence. But our question at the moment is not whether organization or order is permissible in some mode, but whether Jesus in certain basal instances laid down the mode; whether He decreed a constitution for His Church to the measure at least of designating its major officers or ministers. It is His doing of this I find it hard to conceive; on the contrary I more naturally think of Jesus as planting a seed that grew; orders of ministers and sacraments I can regard as proper within that growth, so from Him creatively, begotten of His spirit, though not of Him formally. The Ministry is emergent from Him, of His essential will, rather than set up by Him of specific intent. This, I am saying, is what promptly occurs

---

[1] *The Quest of the Historical Jesus*, p. 401 (the concluding words).

when my thought is turned to the relation of Jesus to the Church and its institutions. It is a view widely shared by those who have come the liberal or liberal-evangelical way in modern theology and Biblical study.

But the view must run the gauntlet of facts. If we can know of things Jesus actually did in the direction of forming a Ministry, then this must have precedence of our *a priori* ideas of what He would be likely to do. And that He did take certain steps this way, it seems impossible to doubt.

There is first His commissioning of the Twelve disciples, narrated in these texts:

Mk. 3: 7ff.:
    Jesus withdrew Himself with His disciples to the sea . . .
    And He goeth up into a mountain, and calleth unto Him whom He would . . .
    And He ordained Twelve, that they should be with Him, and that He might send them forth to preach.

Mt. 10: 1ff.:
    And when He had called unto Him His twelve disciples, He gave them power against unclean spirits . . .
    These twelve Jesus sent forth and commanded them, saying,
    Go not into the way of the Gentiles, and into any city of the Samaritans enter ye not:
    But go rather to the lost sheep of the house of Israel.
    And as ye go, preach, saying, The kingdom of heaven is at hand.

Lk. 9: 1ff.:
    Then He called His twelve disciples together, and gave them power and authority over all devils, and to cure diseases.
    And He sent them to preach the kingdom of God, and to heal the sick. . . .
    And they departed, and went through the towns, preaching the Gospel, and healing everywhere.

This account is plain. Jesus did from among His followers name Twelve and call them apart for a distinct task, or to share the special Kingdom task with Him. Thereby He did in fact create a Ministry, whatever His general attitude toward orders of Ministers. We shall come to other kindred acts of Jesus; and what we, laying predilections aside, have to ask is, Was this activity on His part studied and deliberate, coming of purpose in His mind to provide for His Church an authoritative Ministry? Or is it open to other understanding?

It is of first importance in thinking on this problem to note how Jesus, as the New Testament throughout, conceived the relation both of Himself and the Community that sprang from Him to the race of Israel, the Old Testament People of God. The conception is twofold: on the one hand, Jesus brings judgment to Israel; on the other, the Community He established is itself Israel, the New Israel that continues and fulfils the Old. The judgment purges the Old to make ready for the New. It is the second side of this double relation, the Church the continuation of and the real abiding Israel, that is material to our present question.

A terminological thread gives a first clue to it. *Qahal* (קהל), one of the words in the Hebrew Old Testament for the Congregation of Israel, is commonly rendered ἐκκλησία in the Septuagint (LXX), the Greek version of the Old Testament. This usage reappears in the Greek New Testament: in Acts 7: 38, where Stephen uses ἐκκλησία of the Old Testament Community; and in Heb. 2: 12, where ἐκκλησία occurs in citation from Ps. 21: 23 of the Septuagint, and corresponds to *Qahal* in the equal Hebrew text of Ps. 22: 22. More important as to ἐκκλησία in the New Testament is the taking over of the term by Christians as the name for their own Assembly or Community. In the English versions, ἐκκλησία in this Christian reference is translated by 'Church.' The thread then is: *Qahal*— ἐκκλησία—Church, and it suggests, by this community of terms at different stages, the matter presently in our mind: Christianity's or the Christian Church's accession to God's ordainment for Israel, the continuity of the Divine Order in the Old Testament and in the New.

Numerous texts in the New Testament assert explicitly this continuity; here are examples:

Acts 3: 12, 25, 26:
> Ye men of Israel . . . Ye are the children of the prophets, and of the covenant . . .
>
> Unto you first God, having raised up His Son Jesus, sent Him to bless you . . .

Gal. 3: 13, 14, 16, 17, 29:
> Christ hath redeemed us from the curse of the law . . .
>
> That the blessing of Abraham might come on the Gentiles through Jesus Christ; that we might receive the promise of the Spirit through faith.
>
> Now to Abraham and his seed were the promises made. He saith not, And to seeds, as of many; but as of one, And to thy seed, which is Christ.
>
> And this I say, that the covenant, that was confirmed before of God in Christ, the law cannot disannul . . .
>
> If ye be Christ's, then are ye Abraham's seed, and heirs according to the promise.

I Peter 2: 5, 9:
> Ye also, as living stones, are built up a spiritual house, an holy priesthood . . .
>
> But ye are a chosen generation, a royal priesthood, an holy nation, a peculiar people . . .

In the first of these passages, appeal is made to the "men of Israel" to find their place in God's purpose and their covenant fulfilment in acknowledging Christ and receiving the favour God proffers to them through Him. In the second, Paul blends the New Testament Church with Israel to the full extent of making Gentile Christians equally with Jewish of the seed of Abraham; they are inheritors of the promises made to Abraham and of the hopes arising from them. In the Petrine reference, the phrases in which the members of the Church are addressed are borrowed from the Old Testament, in particular from Ex. 19: 5, 6 which reads: "If ye will obey my voice and keep my covenant, then ye shall be a peculiar treasure unto me above all people . . . And ye shall be unto me a kingdom of priests, and an holy nation." The writer of I Peter takes the very characters of the Old Testament elect people as the Lord Himself here names them and appropriates them to the new Elect of God in Jesus Christ.

These sayings from the New Testament, with many others to like effect which it records, leave us no qualms in accepting this summary word of Dr. Flew: "From the beginning the early Christians regard themselves as the true Israel, inheriting all the promises of God made through the prophets";[1] or this fuller one from Dr. Streeter:

> The first Christians did not regard themselves as a new society but as the ancient "People of God," that is, as that portion of the Church of the Patriarchs and Prophets which had not, by rejecting the Messiah, forfeited its birthright and cut itself off from the "promises of Israel" . . . The Christian position was that by recognizing Jesus as Messiah, they and they alone understood the prophets aright. The number of Jews who had rejected the Messiah was larger than might have been expected, so was the number of the Gentiles who had accepted Him; but that did not alter the fundamental position that only the community of those who did accept Him could claim to be the "Israel of God."[2]

Such, then, the belief of the followers of Jesus. But our interest in referring to this matter turns more directly on the outlook of Jesus Himself. Was it His mind as well as theirs to correlate God's purpose in Him and His call to His ancient people? We look again to the Record, this time to Jesus' own words:

Mk. 1: 15:
The time is fulfilled, and the kingdom of God is at hand.

Mk. 10: 45:
The Son of Man came not to be ministered unto, but to minister, and to give His life a ransom for many (cf. Isa. 53: 11, 12: By his knowledge shall my righteous servant justify many; for he shall bear their iniquities . . . He hath poured out his soul unto death: and he bare the sin of many).

[1] *Jesus and His Church*, p. 139.
[2] *The Primitive Church*, pp. 47, 48.

Lk. 4: 16-21:

> And He came to Nazareth . . . and went into the synagogue
> and stood up for to read.
> And there was delivered unto Him the book of the prophet
> Esaias. And . . . He found the place where it was written,
> The Spirit of the Lord is upon me . . .
> And He began to say unto them, This day is this Scripture
> fulfilled in your ears.

Lk. 22: 37:

> For I say unto you, that this that is written must yet be
> accomplished in me. And he was reckoned among the
> transgressors: for the things concerning me have an end.

Mt. 19: 28 (Lk. 22: 30):

> And Jesus said unto them, Verily I say unto you, That ye
> which have followed me, in the regeneration when the
> Son of Man shall sit in the throne of His glory, ye also
> shall sit upon twelve thrones, judging the twelve tribes
> of Israel.

In these texts Jesus announces the imminent fulfilment
of the visions and expectations Old Testament prophecy
had inspired; they are being or are to be fulfilled in Him
and in the fulfilment the disciples are to share. He thus
links Himself to Old Testament prophecy determinately,
putting Himself in the direct line; but not as one more
prophet, another in the succession (the law and the prophets
were until John: Lk. 16: 16), but as the One in whom the
insights of prophecy are being actualized. He draws to Himself all former aspiration and testimony concerning God's
destiny for Israel, being certain that the great spiritual
issues in the history of Israel are culminating to their crisis
in Him. In particular the Suffering Servant, the greatest of
the prophetic ideals, has in Him stepped out from prophecy
into history and is transposed from ideality into personal
Fact. (Bultmann leaves us unpersuaded that " the tradition
of Jesus' sayings reveals no trace of a consciousness on His
part of being the Servant of God of Isa. 53 ".)[1]

---

[1] *Theology of the New Testament*, I, p. 31.

There is much more in Jesus to show His understanding of the divine part in Israel's course and its purport for Himself. Great strength was afforded Him in the hopes God had given to Israel and from His discerning of the way Israel had been led. For the needs of His own spirit He drew from deep wells of Old Testament religious faith. He taught and commanded love to God and man in the very form in which Israel had been taught before Him (Mt. 22: 37-39; Deut. 6: 4, 5; Lev. 19: 18). His work was to carry forward to its perfect end what God through Moses and the prophets had begun.

Thus Jesus Himself, no less than those who followed Him, joined His own mission to God's dispensation to Israel. More than this: Jesus not only shared the belief of His followers that they were God's chosen community, but He was the fount of this belief. They held it on His authority; in His mind lay the roots and sanctions of it.

Our glance, however, at the way Jesus related Himself to the Old Testament order was for the light it might afford on His intention in choosing and setting apart the Twelve. What help, then, does it yield?

There are familiar precedents in the history of Israel to this act of Jesus; one thinks at once of the Twelve Patriarchs and the Twelve Tribes. But a closer model is given in this Scripture:

> Num. 1: 1-17:
>
> And the Lord spake unto Moses . . .
>
> Take ye the sum of all the congregation of the children of Israel . . . all that are able to go to war in Israel thou and Aaron shalt number by their armies.
>
> And with you there shall be a man of every tribe; every one head of the house of his fathers.
>
> And these are the names of the men that shall stand with you [then *twelve* names, one for each tribe: vv. 5-15].
>
> These were the renowned of the congregation, princes of the tribes of their fathers . . .
>
> And Moses and Aaron took these men which are expressed by their names.

The correspondences between this charge to Moses and Jesus' calling of the disciples are almost exact. God commands Moses to take Twelve, whose names are given, to "stand with him" in the direction of the Israelitish tribes. Jesus takes Twelve to be "with Him" (Mk. 3: 14-19); they also are named (vv. 16-19), and the judging of the "twelve tribes of Israel" is appointed to them (Mt. 19: 28; Lk. 22: 30). Is Jesus, then, in choosing the Twelve making Moses His prototype and carrying His general relating of Himself to Israel to the simple copying of it?

It will reveal His act as something very different from this if we reflect on the actual manner in which Jesus gleaned tokens of the divine will for Him from God's working in the past of His nation. It is this that gives the parallel between Jesus and Moses its true meaning. Jesus was no imitator, of Moses or of any one; but neither was He mere innovator, with no feeling for background. He stood within a *Paradosis* that brought God's former things down the stream of history to blend with the things God was about to do in Him; He realized with deep abiding assurance the oneness of His own advent amongst men with God's other Acts along that stream that had been revelatory and redemptive. What wonder then if, thus looking before and after, He should deem it appropriate or even incumbent upon Him to ordain Twelve to be trained for ministry and responsibility under His hand?

The Twelve Patriarchs, the Twelve Tribes, the Twelve Mosaic Princes . . . the Twelve Apostles; forget the recurring arithmetic save as symbolizing the essential continuum. It is no sign of greatness to scorn symbols, but to divine their significance and through proper use of them to reveal it. Jesus derived much from those who came before Him, from their comprehension of God's ways; His creativity lay, not in starting *ex nihilo* or from *tabula rasa*—one cannot be in history and do that—but in His discriminative adaptation, to His own great ends, of what He thus received. He had come from God to man, not to do despite to time and history, the sphere of man; He had come into the heart of it. Hence His taking up of types or even numbers hallowed

46

in earlier 'divine-human encounters' and through the pilgrimage of faith, is not naïve borrowing but something wholly different; it attests powerfully His acceptance of His place and part in God's historical purpose. If Jesus was to accomplish the reality of the Covenant and Kingdom of which the older divine economy was, in the language of the writer to the Hebrews, the shadow, a shadow, however, carrying the foregleams of the New He would consecrate; then would not the forms of the Old provide, as nothing else could, a reference frame for His Vocation and lines of approach to it? What better signature than these forms pertaining to the temporal Israel could there be, for Him who came to the lost sheep of that same Israel, to bring through them the true Israel into being?

The institution of the Twelve is the salient of these forms. In choosing Twelve Jesus accepts the mission God has now confirmed to Him (Mk. 1: 11); *the choice discloses His intuition of the order of God in history as the meaning of His own presence in the world, and His complete self-identification with that order as emanating from this intuition.* God raised up the tribes and princes of Israel; they and the prophets and other leaders He gave them were His Apostolate under the earlier sign. Jesus in ordaining the Twelve renews the Apostolate, God's sending of men forth that His Word and Will might be known and His Kingdom at last gathered. In this renewal Jesus fulfils —and in doing this "taketh away"—the first Apostolate in answering God's call to "establish" the second (Heb. 10: 9).

On our question, then, Did Jesus in commissioning the Twelve institute a Ministry? we can say at this point: He did create an Apostolate, send out Apostles as God sent the prophets; and we have only to suppose Him to have willed the continuance of this Apostolate to impute to His intention some mode of permanent Ministry.

The appointing of the Twelve, however, is not the only act attributed to Jesus that could mark both the influence upon Him of Jewish institutional practice and His desire to give a Ministry to His Church. For another our text is Lk. 10: 1:

> After these things the Lord appointed other Seventy also, and sent them two by two before His face into every city and place, whither He Himself would come.

This too parallels a Mosaic provision, again in the Book of Numbers: ch. 11, 4-17:

> And the mixt multitude that was among them fell a lusting: and the children of Israel also wept again, and said, Who shall give us flesh to eat?
>
> We remember the fish, which we did eat in Egypt freely; the cucumbers, and the melons . . .
>
> But now our soul is dried away: there is nothing at all, beside this manna . . .
>
> And the Lord said unto Moses, Gather unto me seventy men of the elders of Israel, whom thou knowest to be the elders of the people, and officers over them; and bring them unto the tabernacle of the congregation, that they may stand there with thee.
>
> And I will come down and talk with thee there: and I will take of the spirit which is upon thee, and will put it upon them; and they shall bear the burden of the people with thee, that thou bear it not thyself alone.

This passage shows that in the Mosaic plan for administering the theocratic community, to the Twelve Princes of Num. 1: 1ff. there were added Seventy Elders. Is Jesus then in appointing Seventy following His call of the Twelve, making use of this order of Moses, just stepping in his path? What Moses did belongs to his re-constituting of Israel by the covenant. Jesus has come for another re-constituting of the People under a new covenant. Is it His mind as to the form of this to adhere measure by measure to what Moses had given?

In regard to the Twelve, we have already seen cause for denying that Jesus was imitating Moses; notwithstanding that we found a relation of Jesus to Moses or to the history linked with his name that was to Jesus deeply meaningful.

In the instance of the Seventy we can also reject mere copying, but in other ways the sending forth of the Seventy is not so simple. That it rests as surely as the naming of the Twelve on a specific act of Jesus cannot so confidently be assumed. The Twelve continue in connection with Jesus throughout the Gospel history; of the Seventy no more is heard beyond an allusion to their return from their mission in the same chapter (v. 17) that narrates their being charged with it. It has been held that the tradition of the Seventy figures forth Christianity's mission to the Gentiles as the Twelve signalized that to the Jews. Jesus commanded the Twelve: " Go not in the way of the Gentiles . . . go to the lost sheep of Israel" (Mt. 10: 5, 6). Taking this view, the inclusion of the sending out of the Seventy in the Third Gospel serves to presage, as from the time of Jesus Himself and consonantly with His own wider purpose, the Church's widening frontiers marked out by Luke in his other writing when it had become confirmed to the Christian mind that God had destined Christianity for other peoples, not for Israel only. This points to a further affinity of the Lucan Seventy and the Seventy Elders appointed by Moses; for this appointment also was for the Gentiles, the " mixt multitude " of Num. 11: 4 (cf. Ex. 12: 38), distinguished from the children of Israel (note in the reference " the children of Israel also ") though in company with them.

This phase of the subject of the 'Seventy' will have meanings for us in a later context. In our immediate interest, the suggestion that for the understanding of the Seventy of Lk. 10: 1 we look beyond the Gospels to developments in the Church of the Acts of the Apostles would seem to tell against making the Seventy a principal guidepost in our search for what Jesus did toward establishing a Ministry. For such guidance we must still look to His calling of the Twelve disciples, not only since it can, more certainly than the sending of the Seventy, be placed among the things Jesus actually did, but because, touching the whole question of His mind in respect of the Ministry, it is on any reading of the Gospels the signal step in all that is recorded of Him.

D

In regard to the choosing of the Twelve we have already concluded: Jesus did by this choice, from a purpose that was all-essential to Him, name and set apart those who would be in a special way His servants and helpers in the Kingdom work. His act was simple and unadorned in comparison to the Church's later style in making and designating orders of Ministers; nonetheless was a Ministry inaugurated by it, an Apostolic Ministry since the Ministers were Apostles, those sent by Him.

Proceeding from this conclusion we come next to the nature and offices of the Ministry Jesus thus called into being.

First is the office of preaching. The Twelve were chosen to be with Jesus and to be sent out to preach (Mk. 3: 14). To preach the Word has always had " honour of place " in the ministerial calling. Ministers are preachers of the Gospel if they are anything; the first Ministers unquestionably were made such by Jesus Himself (Mt. 10: 7; Lk. 8: 1; 9: 2; cf. Mk. 16: 15).

But in other places in the Record Jesus seems to add to preaching other functions or even prerogatives that are not so universally or inevitably regarded as pertaining to the Ministry; instead they have been a stone of stumbling and difficulty and a cause of discord and division in the Church's ranks. We refer to such texts as these:

Mt. 16: 19:
I will give unto thee the keys of the kingdom of heaven; and whatsoever thou shalt bind on earth shall be bound in heaven; and whatsoever thou shalt loose on earth shall be loosed in heaven.

John 20: 21-23:
Then said Jesus to them again, Peace be unto you: as my Father hath sent me, even so send I you.
And when He had said this, He breathed on them, and saith unto them, Receive ye the Holy Ghost:
Whose soever sins ye remit, they are remitted unto them; and whose soever sins ye retain, they are retained.

Jesus here lays a charge upon the Apostles that is solemn and tremendous beyond all thought. What does it mean that men are given this power, to bind and loose, to remit or retain sins?

One thing these texts make clear is that this power bestowed upon the Apostles is bound up with their relationship to Christ. In the first passage the words we have set down, as they occur in the Gospel narrative, are spoken to Peter in consequence of his confession of Christ, which has sprung not from his own insight but from God's testimony to him concerning Christ (vv. 16, 17). In the second the Spirit, empowering to remit or retain sins, comes to the Apostles as those sent by Christ even as Christ was sent.

This being sent—of Christ as Christ was sent of God—is the essence of Apostleship and defines Apostolic Ministry (Apostle is ἀπόστολος 'one sent'; verbal form ἀποστέλλω to send or dispatch). But 'sent' in Biblical usage has a singular meaning, and a consideration of this will cast light on the matter now before us, the thought in the mind of Jesus when He spoke of His Ministers as forgiving or retaining sins, and the dependence of their power to forgive on their community with Him.

This special meaning of 'sent' is met first in the Old Testament in the frequent force of *shalach* (שָׁלַח), the Hebrew correspondent to ἀποστέλλω, and in the nominal *shaliach* (שָׁלִיחַ), the equivalent of ἀπόστολος. The meaning is special in the way in which in referring to one sent (*shaliach*) it disposes the persons of the 'sent' and the sender. A householder sends a member of his household who is received *as* the householder; through his agency in the business on which he is sent the householder himself acts. Such agents are "extensions of their master's personality and are treated as actually being and not merely representing their lord."[1] This identity of sent and sender has its conspicuous case in the Old Testament prophet who, as sent of God, is not only seen by others but presents himself as one in whom God Himself has come. His word is not " I [under divine

[1] Johnson, *The One and the Many in the Israelite Conception of God*, p. 10.

instruction] say unto you," but "Thus saith the Lord." Or
as in these examples:

> I Sam. 15: 1:
>> The Lord sent me to anoint thee to be king . . . now, there-
>> fore, hearken [not to me but] unto the voice of the
>> words of the Lord.

> Jer. 7: 25, 26:
>> I have sent unto you all my servants the prophets . . . yet
>> they hearkened not unto [not them but] me.

This character of the 'sent' (*shaliach*) as one with the
sender continues through the whole Jewish period, and for
all sorts of instances of sender and sent. "A man's *shaliach*
is the man himself" is a proverbial Rabbinic saying, cited
repeatedly in the Talmud. But central to our interest is the
similar expression of the unity of sender and sent in connection with ἀπόστολος, the Greek parallel of *shaliach*.
This is not unknown to secular and classical usage, but its
consummate form is in the New Testament and has to do
with our present topic, the relation of Jesus to those sent
out by Him. We insert the following in proof of this:

> Mt. 10: 2, 5, 19, 20, 40:
>> Now the names of the twelve apostles are these . . .
>> These twelve Jesus sent forth, and commanded them . . .
>> When they deliver you up, take no thought how or what
>> ye shall speak: for it shall be given you in that same
>> hour what ye shall speak.
>> For it is not ye that speak, but the Spirit of your Father
>> which speaketh in you.
>> He that receiveth you receiveth me, and he that receiveth
>> me receiveth Him that sent me.

> Lk. 10: 16:
>> He that heareth you heareth me; and he that despiseth
>> you despiseth me; and he that despiseth me despiseth
>> Him that sent me.

> John 5: 30; 14: 10; 15: 15; 17: 23; 20: 21:
>> I can of mine own self do nothing . . . I seek not mine own
>> will, but the will of the Father which hath sent me.

I am in the Father, and the Father in me: the words that
I speak unto you I speak not of myself: but the Father
that dwelleth in me, He doeth the works.

All things that I have heard of my Father I have made
known unto you.

I in them, and thou in me, that they may be made perfect
in one; and that the world may know that thou hast
sent me . . .

As my Father hath sent me, even so send I you.

These texts need no commentary to establish that the
New Testament Apostle has *shaliach* character and
authority as genuinely as the Old Testament prophet. " It
is not ye that speak, but the spirit . . . speaketh in you; he
that heareth, receiveth you, receiveth, heareth me "—what
could be plainer? As was the prophet to God so is the
Apostle to Christ; or even more, the comparison being of
Christ's sending of the Apostles and God's sending of Christ,
the oneness of the Apostle with Christ is the oneness, not of
the prophet, but of Christ Himself with God (" I in them
and thou in me "). Christ sent of God is God's *shaliach* who
is God Himself (" I of mine own self do nothing; I seek not
mine own will but the will of Him that sent me; the Father
that dwelleth in me doeth the works "). The Apostles in
similar manner (" as the Father hath sent me so I send
you ") are Christ's *shaliach*, their word not their own but
His, as His is not His own but God's (note precision of
parallel in the above passages: " I speak not of myself "
. . . " It is not ye that speak "). We can easily overstrain
these correspondences. Jesus' people are not of His essence
as, in Catholic theology, He and the Father are of one
being. But in mission and witness the Apostles were " as
He " in the world (I John 4: 17); truth and authority were
in them as in Him, being from Him. Their coming to men
was not in His name only but—the distinctive force of the
shaliach-idea—in His Person; as in Him God came in
Person. Thus was " *He* in them as the Father in Him "; " all
things He heard of the Father He made known to them."

We have introduced this *shaliach* principle at this stage
for its possible bearing on Christ's authorizing of His

Apostles to remit or retain sins. The principle figures much in discussions of the Ministry, though judgments vary concerning its value. Our own summary word will come later; suffice at present this one connection of the principle. We can learn this connection from Paul who definitely claimed for his ministry the *shaliach* quality. "The Sender present with the sent" could hardly have plainer exemplification than in "I live, yet not I, but Christ liveth in me" (Gal. 2: 20); or than when Paul writes, "We are ambassadors . . . as though God did beseech by us: we pray you in Christ's stead" (2 Cor. 5: 20). But Paul has in this latter Epistle (2: 10) another word: "If I forgave anything . . . forgave I it in the *person* (ἐν προσώπῳ) of Christ." These sayings of Paul read conjointly disclose the "tie that binds" the Apostles' forgiving or remitting sins and the *shaliach* relation. The Apostle being Christ's *shaliach*, His person to the extent of his apostleship, forgives in His person; the sent being the Sender acts as He. If Christ "hath authority (ἐξουσία: Mk. 2: 10) on earth to forgive sins," and if authority in His ministers is His gift of *His* authority to them, will they not in employing their authority share His forgiving activity? This issue will be resumed in a later chapter; meanwhile sufficient has been said to confirm our statement that the power of the keys, to bind and loose, however we conceive the precise manner of it, rests with the other powers bestowed on the Apostles on their relationship to Christ; only substance and depth are added to the statement through the cause we have found for expressing the relationship as effectual identity with Christ.

Protestants have sometimes felt dismay, or even anger, over the claims of certain men to be Vicars of Christ. Popes may not be the people; but Vicars of Himself, persons standing for Him, were surely intended by Jesus if His acts and words were as we have presented them. Jesus called a Ministry to be so immediately in His own place that men hearing and receiving would hear and receive Him; He gave this Ministry His own power (Lk. 9: 1). Whence He could say, All power is given unto *me*, and then, not *I* go, but Go *ye* therefore (Mt. 28: 19, 20), a *non sequitur* as the prophet's ' therefore ' in the examples above,[1] save as Christ and His Ministers truly are one potency. Thus it is the Ministry itself, the whole Ministry, that is vicarious, not some ranking portion of it. Jesus named the Apostles and their authority and power, even as their Word, were as Himself in them exerting and extending in the world His very presence. So it remains: to be joined with Christ, not just His representative but to be one with Him in Word and Power, is ever the existence and burden—and singular freedom—of the Apostolic Minister.

We have now considered " what Jesus did toward creating a Ministry " in the two aspects, first of the manner in which Jesus can be said to have established a Ministry, and then of the powers and tasks He ordained for it. Our discussion has leaned toward phases of His purpose and activity which, authentic in themselves, can be viewed as favouring the doctrine of the Ministry presently under our survey. Many of the matters we have touched upon, very notably Christ's gift of the keys, of the power to remit sins, have been variously interpreted and applied in different sections of the Church, and in consequence as we have already hinted will have our attention again. In the meanwhile we turn to other stages in the early growth of the Ministry where further supports have been sought for the Catholic doctrine.

II

The Continuance and Development of the Ministry in the First Centuries of the Church

The evidence of the section just concluded leaves little doubt that the Apostles were ordained by Jesus to a high order of Ministry, embracing the functions necessary for establishing and directing the life of the Church, oversee-

[1] *supra*, p. 52.

ing the fellowship, "strengthening the brethren" (Lk. 22: 32). Jesus willed this Ministry and the appointing of it was His own act. A question that has peeped at us in our progress that we have not stopped to face is, Did Jesus intend this Ministry simply as an auxiliary to Himself in the Kingdom work during His lifetime, or was it His will that it continue as He instituted it throughout the historical life of the Church? Or alternatively again, was its continuance, whether formally envisaged by Him or not, the due historical corollary of what He commanded and did? These questions must now have our thought and we shall seek light upon them from the course of the Ministry in the early Christian centuries, as we try to measure the case for seeing in this course a proper prolongation of what Jesus began or an embodying of further creative action by His Spirit.

The Ministry of the Apostles reappears after the departure of Jesus, and the Apostolate of Twelve is at first so far deemed normative or even essential that Matthias is chosen to fill the place of Judas (Acts 1: 15-26)). Here formally is Apostolic Succession, one numbered with the Apostles whom Jesus did not appoint. The historical line of Ministry, however, does not seem to have passed through Matthias. Other Apostles of greater prominence soon appeared, and the question to be asked is, Are these others the successors of the first Apostles as being chosen and consecrated by them?

By far the most notable is the Apostle Paul. He claims Apostleship in full, the freedom that bespeaks the Apostle's authority, the seal of Apostolicity in a labour whose fruits forbid other appraisal of it (I Cor. 9: 1, 2).

Paul, however, is an Apostle not by men, former Apostles or others, but through the will of God (I Cor. 1: 1). His commission is direct from God: "when it pleased God, who separated me . . . I conferred not with flesh and blood: Neither went I up to them which were Apostles before me" (Gal. 1: 15-17). Paul here seems very far from seeking the proof of his ministry in descent from the original Apostles. He counselled with them, with Peter (Gal. 1: 18, 19), with them all in their assembly (Acts 15: 1ff.); he 'received' the Word which he delivered (I Cor. 15: 3), and he was separated and ordained to his *special* work by those who were already ministers in the Apostolic Church (Acts 13: 1-3). Yet his position taken as a whole places him apart, and there seems good reason for regarding the call of Paul as the direct act of the Lord Himself (Acts 9: 4-6, 15). He is added to the original Apostles rather than a successor of them. This is confirmed when Paul includes the appearance of Jesus to himself among the Resurrection appearances (I Cor. 15: 8) and rests his Apostleship upon it (I Cor. 9: 1). He ranks with the Apostles as sharing their witness to the Resurrection, not through lineage from them.

On our question, then, Are other New Testament Apostles ordained by the first Apostles and have they their office from them? the case of Paul is too singular and untypical to be decisive. He honours the work of the Apostles while asserting his independence of them. He is Apostle by grace only of Jesus Christ (Gal. 1: 1).

But others in the New Testament whose vocation is Apostolic do seem to have their place and calling through Apostolic forebears. Perhaps the most instructive instances are those of Timothy and Titus. Both are 'sons' of 'Paul,' the writer of the Pastoral Epistles (I Tim. 1: 2; 2 Tim. 1: 2; Titus 1: 4). Acts 16: 1-3 tells of Timothy's circumcision by Paul. The 'Paul' of the Pastorals gives to each his commission. To Timothy in the words: "I besought thee to abide at Ephesus . . . that thou mightest charge some that they teach no other doctrine . . . the things thou hast heard of me commit to faithful men, who shall be able to teach others also" (I Tim. 1: 3; 2 Tim. 2: 2); and to Titus: "I left thee in Crete, that thou shouldest set in order the things that are wanting, and ordain elders in every city, as I had appointed thee" (Titus 1: 5).

Timothy and Titus, however, are nowhere named Apostles. Yet the signs abound of the Apostolic character of their office and labours. They are self-evidently Apostolic deputies if it is an Apostle who speaks to them in the words just given. The ministry of the New Testament Apostles

57

seems to have included general oversight of the Church and responsibility for ordaining to other ministries (Acts 6: 6; 14: 14, 23). In both regards Timothy and Titus exercise this ministry: their jurisdiction is general throughout the areas to which they are assigned and they ordain to the local ministries, to the eldership, as in Titus 1: 5 above, and to the diaconate (I Tim. 3: 8ff.). The command to Titus to "ordain elders in every city" conveys both these phases of Apostolic Ministry in one instruction, even as it answers word by word to Apostolic precedent (Acts 14: 14, 23).

The behest to ordain in these texts from the Pastoral Epistles lies in relation to the need for soundness and continuity in word and doctrine. Both of these, the authority to ordain and the maintenance of right doctrine, have been through history predominant Christian concerns, and they figure centrally in the argument for Apostolic Episcopacy; the belief being that Ministry descended from the Apostles will properly bear both the authority and the teaching. This lends interest to the fact that in regard to both, to ordination and doctrine, these writings disclose the importance or even the necessity of sequence and transmission. This is seen, as to the one, in those who are called to ordain having already their own ministry through the laying on of Apostolic hands (2 Tim. 1: 6; cf. I Tim. 4: 14), and in the command to them to appoint in turn "as I had appointed thee" (Titus 1: 5). It appears as to the other in the doctrine having been received from Paul with admonition to commit again to those who will teach (2 Tim. 2: 2).

Is not the genuine thread of Apostolic Succession being here unveiled? Respecting its two essentials, authenticating the teaching and preserving the right to ordain, the Apostle's commission to his 'sons' is their directive also to commission. So the steps multiply: Paul, Timothy, those whom Timothy chooses, those instructed by these. So is begun link by link, to continue unbroken through the centuries, the golden chain of Ministry.

Yet in comparison with the full doctrine of Apostolic Succession, there is one great lack in what these Pastoral Letters have opened to us. This doctrine postulates, not just the

continuance in the Church of Apostolic ministry and testimony, but its procession down the one main channel repre-
sented through most of Christian history by the Catholic
bishops. But Paul, Timothy and Titus, succeed in order as
they may, are not 'bishops' as the New Testament knows
them.

Bishops in the New Testament, the ministers so named,
are not Apostles with their general range of ministration,
but local Church officers, hardly distinguishable from
elders. Many New Testament interpreters identify them
with the elders (presbyters) and speak of presbyter-
bishops (πρεσβύτεροι-ἐπίσκοποι). So in Acts 20: 17, 28: Paul
calls the elders of Ephesus and addresses them as overseers
(ἐπίσκοποι : bishops) of the flock. In Titus 1: 5-7, elders
are to be appointed from among those who are blameless,
"for a *bishop* must be blameless." When we meet two local
Church ministerial orders, they are bishops *or* elders and
deacons (Phil. 1: 1; I Tim. 3: 1-8; cf. *Didache* XV), not
bishops *and* elders. In no instance does one of these occur
collaterally with the other.

There are those, however, who doubt this identity of
bishops and presbyters in the New Testament. 'Episcopoi'
in Acts 20: 28, it is pointed out, is most likely a reference
to the elders' function rather than a formal title. Then
attention is drawn to two things in the Pastoral Epistles:
first, while 'elder' and 'deacon' occur in the plural,
'bishop' is always singular; second, the 'if any' which in
Titus 1: 6 seems to link the elders and the bishop of vv. 5
and 7, is elsewhere in these writings (I Tim. 3: 1; 5: 4, 16;
6: 3) an idiom for introducing a new subject. If it is so here,
then Titus 1: 6 belongs to what follows rather than to what
precedes and disconnects 'elders' (v. 5) and 'bishop' (v. 7)
instead of joining them. "It would appear," writes one who
has weighed these alternatives, "that so far from this passage in Titus providing support for the equation presbyter-
episkopos, it actually denies it."[1] This is going a long way;
but one can at least grant the possibility that Acts 20: 17,
28 and Titus 1: 5-7, the two texts most commonly relied

[1] Jalland, *The Origin and Evolution of the Christian Church*, pp. 68, 69.

upon for the identifying of New Testament elders and bishops, are not as conclusive to this effect as has been thought.

But whatever our mind as to this, we are not long in the period following the Pastoral Letters before, at least in some areas of the Church, the rule has emerged under which bishops and presbyters are distinct and there is in each Church the single bishop who, still a local Church minister, has precedence of other local ministers. This is the condition known as monepiscopacy, and we shall here give our thought to it as a first step in the effort to trace the course by which bishops, from being members of groups of local Church leaders or ministers, attained to such scale and dignity of office and oversight in the general Church that they could appropriately be regarded as standing in the place of the Apostles and continuing their Ministry. This effort is central to this stage of our inquiry.

The beginnings of monepiscopacy may be visible in the New Testament, however we adjudge the above issue respecting the relations of ministers in the Pastoral Epistles. Who, for example, are the angels of the seven Churches, one to each severally, of Revelation 2 and 3? Are they bishops of these Churches? Then " Diotrephes who loveth preeminence " (3 John, v. 9) implies that for some *one* to have preeminence is now a possibility. We know it as a normal practice of directing groups, however in principle composed of equals, to choose a chairman or leader; this case of Diotrephes suggests that this natural ally in the emergence of monepiscopacy is already being abetted by personal ambition. But whatever the actual beginnings, this replacing of the college of elders as the supreme body in the local Church by an individual head, did occur; this head was soon to be if he was not at first called the bishop. If this is not quite certain from the New Testament, it becomes wholly so in writings hardly later than some of its parts.

In illustration, here are passages from the *Letters* of Ignatius which if genuine, and they are widely so received, must have been penned before A.D. 117, the end of the reign of Trajan during which Ignatius suffered martyrdom:

To the Trallians:

For when you are in subjection to the bishop as to Jesus Christ it is clear to me that you are living not after men, but after Jesus Christ . . . Therefore . . . do nothing without the bishop, but be also in subjection to the presbytery . . . Likewise let all respect the deacons as Jesus Christ . . . Without these the name of ' Church ' is not given.

To the Ephesians:

For Jesus our inseparable life, is the will of the Father, even as the bishops, who have been appointed throughout the world, are by the will of Jesus Christ. . . Your justly famous presbytery, worthy of God, is attuned to the bishop as the strings to a harp.

To the Philadelphians:

Be careful therefore to use one Eucharist (for there is one flesh of our Lord Jesus Christ, and one cup of union with His blood, one altar, as there is one bishop with the presbytery and the deacons my fellow-servants), in order that whatever you do you may do it according to God.

To the Smyrnaeans:

See that you all follow the bishop, as Jesus Christ follows the Father, and the presbytery as if it were the Apostles. And reverence the deacons as the command of God. Let no one do anything appertaining to the Church without the bishop. Let that be considered a valid Eucharist which is celebrated by the bishop, or by one whom he appoints. Wherever the bishop appears let the congregation be present; just as wherever Jesus Christ is, there is the Catholic Church. It is not lawful either to baptize or to hold an 'agapé' without the bishop; but whatever he approve, this is pleasing to God, that everything you do may be secure and valid. . . It is good to know God and the bishop.

These transcriptions speak plainly; the bishop as they picture him is unequivocally the singular head and spiritual guide in each congregation. Whether monepiscopacy was, at this early date, as complete in fact as Ignatius' words suggest, there is no reserve in his espousal of it. He meets counter currents in the Church with an unambiguous defence. Noticeable too in these texts is the bishop's *shaliach* place and authority ("when you are in subjection to the bishop *as* to Jesus Christ you are living after Jesus Christ"). "Follow the bishop as Jesus Christ follows the Father" only converts Jesus' "As my Father hath sent me, even so send I you." These paragraphs enshrine also the principle of Succession, in the words just repeated and in these from *To the Ephesians:* "Jesus is the will of the Father, even as the bishops are by the will of Jesus Christ."

One thing, destined to major emphasis in the later formulation of Succession, is not yet explicit: the descent of bishops from the Apostles. Ignatius' parallels vary; the bishop is now as Jesus Christ, now as the Father; the deacons are to be respected as Jesus Christ; presbytery rather than the episcopate is likened to the Apostles. Yet the succession of bishops from the Apostles is latent in Ignatius' thought. He is concerned for order in the Church, and he sees its type and guaranty in bishop and presbyters in corresponding place to Christ and the Apostles. While this directly links the presbyters, not the bishops, to the Apostles, yet the bishop standing as Christ would bear His authority, and as this was first given to the Apostles (Lk. 9 : 1), its transmission to the bishop would naturally come in due course to be regarded as lying through them.

Other things were happening in the Church toward this same end or toward making emphatic in the Church's mind the connection of the bishops with the Apostles. First steps in this advance are seen in another post-Apostolic writing, *The First Epistle of Clement*, possibly of earlier date than the *Epistles* of Ignatius. Here are the important sections:

> *I Clement* 42 :
> The Apostles received the Gospel for us from the Lord Jesus Christ. Jesus the Christ was sent from God. So then Christ is from God and the Apostles from Christ. Both come by the will of God in the appointed order. Having therefore received their commands, and being fully assured

62

by the resurrection of our Lord Jesus Christ, and with faith confirmed by the Word of God, they went forth in the assurance of the Holy Spirit preaching the Gospel. . . . They preached from district to district, and from city to city, and they appointed their first converts, testing them by the Spirit, to be bishops and deacons of the future believers.

I Clement 44:

Our Apostles also knew through our Lord Jesus Christ that there would be strife for the title of bishop. For this cause, since they had received perfect foreknowledge, they appointed those who have been mentioned, and afterwards added this enactment that if they should fall asleep, other approved men should succeed to their ministry (λειτουργία). We consider, therefore, that it is not just to remove from their ministry those who were appointed by them, or later by other eminent men, with the consent of the whole Church.

The situation reflected in these paragraphs may in some aspects be less mature than in Ignatius. "Bishops and deacons" being appointed by the Apostles as they "preach from city to city" points back to Acts 14: 23 and to the condition where bishops (interchangeably with elders) and deacons are the dual local ministry (Phil. 1: 1). On the other hand, "there is strife for the title of bishop" implies that the separation of bishop and presbyter, if not as complete as in Ignatius, has so far emerged that the role of the bishop as *primus inter pares* of the presbyters has become covetable. On our immediate question of the relation of the bishops to the Apostles, Clement is slightly more specific than Ignatius in placing the bishops in the line from the Apostles. Writing to a practical end, to quell dissension in the Corinthian Church, he pictures bishops (and other ministers) as chosen by the Apostles with the injunction to choose in turn that others might be ready as the need occurred. This is Ministry in continuing Succession from the Apostles as it could naturally have arisen. Clement in speaking of it is not conscious of innovating but writes to a strain that assumes it as already familiar. Yet what he says looks to the future as well as to the past and present. For it is in the period following Clement and Ignatius that Succession, in principle as Clement has instanced it, is explored as to its meaning for the character of the Ministry, and the idea of Succession approaches the place history is keeping for it in the Church's life and belief.

For full understanding of this, however, we must take into account another transforming change in the order of Episcopacy and its place in the Church. So far our thought has centred on the stages by which plurality of bishops as local Church administrators slowly yielded to the Ignatian monepiscopos, and on the contingent issue of the bishop's position with respect to the Apostles. This further transformation is of a different sort; it is the one whereby the province of the bishop, from being the particular congregation or the Church in one city, was enlarged to include a measure of care of the Churches of adjacent areas. This marks the beginnings of the diocesan and the metropolitan episcopate, with all it held for future developments of Church order and of thought and doctrine pertaining to it.

It is not difficult to conjecture how these beginnings arose, in the spontaneity with which the bishop in such a centre as Antioch or Ephesus would be looked to by the smaller neighbourhood Churches. Again there are foreshowings in the New Testament. James from the Great Church in Jerusalem exerts a sway beyond its precincts (Acts 15); he, however, may be regarded as, like Paul, added to the first Apostles. More suggestive or prophetic of the diocesan relation as it emerged is 3 John, whose writer purposes to visit, perhaps from Ephesus, and to act with authority in, the Church where already he has reproved Diotrephes (vv. 9, 10). This tendency to central direction or oversight would increase as Christianity spread; and it would be natural, as belief in episcopal descent from the Apostles grew in the Church, that the bishop exercising this central office rather than as simply the local Church head, still more those at the great centres whose jurisdiction would approximate yet more nearly to the general one of the Apostles, would be specially identified with the Apostolate. When about A.D. 175 Hegesippus, one of the earliest Church historians, states formally the principle of Succession, this identification has occurred; the trend has arisen toward finding in the larger Sees the centre of the Apostolic Commission.

The need for this Commission and for certainty of its whereabouts had now become imperative through new strains the Church was undergoing. A crisis was gathering that was to involve Christianity's very substance. This crisis has importance for us as yielding a further stage in the conception and growth of Apostolic Ministry. The early believers had their anchorage in the Apostles' doctrine (Acts 2: 42). But the Apostles passed, and as yet there was no authoritative repository of their teaching. The New Testament as a *corpus* of Scripture was in the making, the Church's decision as to the Canon lying far in the future. On the other hand, the Old Testament had long been extant as Scripture; it was 'the Scriptures' to Jesus and the Apostles. It came quite naturally that the commonly received Scriptures in the first age of the Church were those of the Old Testament. In the sub-apostolic period the Church drew largely from the ethical aspects of Old Testament religion; with the consequence of a deviation of the Church's mind toward Judaic moralism and a weakened grasp of Redemptive Grace as in Paul and the New Testament throughout. But a people that had 'tasted' salvation-religion could not long stay assuaged with law and ethics. The age thirsted for hope, and the letting slip of the Apostolic Gospel left the door wide for 'another' (Gal. 1: 8) to flow into the breach. Gnosticism was to hand and was nothing loth; and soon the stake was Christianity's very being, through the alternative Gospel of *Gnosis* claiming diviner assurance and promising higher spiritual rewards than Faith (πίστις) grounded in the Evangelical Facts.

There were strong leaders in the Church who truly felt the issue. The true Gospel, they declared, must stand against this tide threatening to engulf it. But by what rule could they identify and certify this Gospel with the New Testament as we possess it not in their hands? We found in the Pastoral Epistles the maintenance of the Gospel entrusted to a continuing Ministry: the writer would have his "dearly beloved son" choose those to come after him and prepare them to teach "in faith and verity no other doctrine" (I Tim. 1: 3; 2: 7; 2 Tim. 2: 2). He must do this the more that others are forsaking the Gospel for the oppositions of "*gnosis* falsely so called" (I Tim. 6: 20; 2 Tim. 4: 3). We may see here the incipient phase of the condition we are noticing; and already the instrument of its correction is the word of an Apostle passing from hand to hand. The Church was to follow along this path. Her leaders turned the edge of Gnosticism by directing her for guidance to Churches that had been the scene of an Apostle's ministry, or where appointees of the Apostles or others who had derived from them still laboured and taught. Who if not these, the bishops in these Churches, would have maintained the faith given to the Apostles and be heirs of their authority? So the vacuum in the Church's life till the New Testament could be formed was bridged, through the ministry of bishops in succession from the Apostles; the Church could have recourse to these bishops for the norms and for authentication of her belief. This was the confidence, for example, of Irenaeus toward the end of the second century, in one of the great classic enunciations of Apostolic Episcopal Succession. We give the text of it:

Irenaeus, *Adversus Haereses*, III. iii, 1-3:
The tradition of the Apostles, made manifest in all the world, all may look back upon, who wish to see things truly; and we are able to recount those whom the Apostles appointed to be bishops in the Churches, and their successors, even down to us . . . Very perfect and blameless would they have them to be, whom they were leaving to be their actual successors . . . But because it were very long to reckon up the successions in all the Churches, there is one, very great, and most ancient and known to all the Church founded and established at Rome by two most glorious Apostles, Peter and Paul, whose tradition which it hath from the Apostles, and her faith proclaimed unto men by succession of bishops coming down to us, we point

to . . . The blessed Apostles, then, having founded and builded the Church, committed the ministry of the Episcopate to Linus (2 Tim. 4: 21) . . . And his successor is Anenclitus: and after him in the third place from the Apostles . . . Clement, who had both seen the blessed Apostles, and conferred with them, and had the doctrine of the Apostles yet sounding in his ears, and their tradition before his eyes . . . By the same order, and in the same succession, both the tradition from the Apostles in the Church, and the preaching of the truth, have come down to us.

IV. xxvi, 2, 5:
Wherefore we should hearken to those elders who are in the Church; those who have the succession in the Episcopate received a sure gift of truth, at the good pleasure of the Father . . . Where, therefore, the gifts of the Lord have been placed, there it behoves us to learn the truth, from those who possess that succession in the Church which is from the Apostles, and among whom exists that which is sound and blameless in conduct, as well as that which is unadulterated and incorrupt in speech.

IV. xxxiii, 8:
True *gnosis* is the teaching of the Apostles, and the original system of the Church in the whole world, and the mark of Christ's body in the several successions of the bishops to whom they committed that Church, which is in each several place.

So spake Irenaeus to the Church in one of her testing epochs. He is aflame for the Evangel, the *Kerygma* of the Apostles, as he sees the Church being invaded by falsifications of it. But the Church is asking, "To whom shall we go" for the Evangel? Irenaeus' answer was the surest that could then be given: the Ministry closest in derivation from the Apostles would have received the Evangel from them; to this Ministry bearing "the doctrine of the Apostles" the Church can repair for her Word. "Sound doctrine" we have seen was the interest that underlay Succession as informally enjoined in the Pastoral Epistles (I Tim. 1: 3; 2 Tim. 2: 2); Apostolic Episcopal Succession is confirmed as guarantor of doctrine through its more overt adoption by Irenaeus and those who think with him. Down the centuries to our own day, Episcopal Succession has been extolled as continuing this same high service. "The Church of England is an episcopal Church and does not regard episcopacy merely as a convenient form of government, but also as the guarantee of continuity in Apostolic teaching and administration."[1]

The Church's dependence for the establishment of her Word on bishops in cities associated in tradition with the Apostles, was a prime agent in the further fashioning of Church order and the Ministry which we remarked above as foretokened in the extension of the bishop's rule from the local to a more general range. This dependence was effectual in this way through its results for the Episcopate itself both in its character and work. Called to voice the Faith for the whole Christian Body divided and distracted over the very nature of it, the Episcopal Ministry would be set in fair course to resume in full the vocation of the Apostles and their place in the Church (Acts 2: 42). The records of the age show a definite trend toward joining to this Ministry the distinctive Apostolic qualities and duties. We have seen this trend in Ignatius and at a marked stage in Irenaeus; what these reveal as in process comes very close to formal completeness in another work, the *Didascalia Apostolorum*, a third century Greek text most familiar to modern students in a Syriac translation. It purports to come from the Apostles, who in the course of it admonish the bishops, giving them this charge:

Didascalia VII:
> Do thou, O Bishop, teach and rebuke, and loose by forgiveness. And know thy place, that it is that of God Almighty, and that thou hast received authority to forgive sins. For to you bishops it was said: All that ye shall bind on earth shall be bound in heaven; and all that ye shall loose shall be loosed. As therefore thou hast authority to loose, know thyself and thy manners and thy conversation in this life, that they may be worthy of thy place.

[1] Garbett, *The Claims of the Church of England*, p. 93.

This passage does several things. It perfects the *shaliach* quality of the Ministry—"know thy place that it is that of God." Touching the matter now before us, it imports in full the identity of the bishops with the Apostles, not only in presenting the Apostles as laying on the bishops their own charge, but in the straight assertion to the bishops that the words about binding and loosing which Jesus spoke to the Apostles (Mt. 16: 19; 18: 18) were said to them. The passage also reproduces the New Testament connection of the *shaliach* order of Ministry and other Apostolic offices; in particular, binding and loosing are *shaliach* powers and duties ("thy place is that of God, thou hast authority to forgive"), conformably again to Paul's forgiving in the *Person* of Christ (2 Cor. 2: 10) and to John 20: 21, 23 where they who 'remit' are the 'sent' as Christ was 'sent.'

The unity of Bishops and Apostles is manifest in another early third century work, *The Apostolic Tradition* of Hippolytus. Witness its *Prayer for the Consecration of a Bishop*:

> O God and Father of our Lord Jesus Christ . . .
> Who didst give ordinances unto Thy Church by the word of Thy grace; Who didst foreordain from the beginning the race of the righteous from Abraham, instituting princes and priests and leaving not Thy sanctuary without ministers . . .
> Pour forth that power which is from Thee, of the princely Spirit, which He bestowed on Thy holy Apostles who established the Church . . .
> Father who knowest the hearts of all, grant upon this Thy servant whom Thou hast chosen for the episcopate to feed Thy holy flock and serve as Thine high priest, that he may minister blamelessly by night and day . . . and offer to Thee the gifts of Thy holy Church,
> And that by the high priestly Spirit he may have authority to forgive sins according to the command . . . to "loose every bond" which Thou gavest to the Apostles . . .

In these words again the identity of Bishops and Apostles is evinced in the power to 'loose' and forgive bestowed by Christ on the Apostles being held proper to the bishop and besought for him. Hippolytus writes as the Church is approaching another crisis in which Apostolic-Episcopacy will once more have crucial part. His contemporary, Cyprian of Carthage, is concerned that Christians, under stress of persecution, be united lest Christianity be destroyed; and he sees the Episcopate as through its own unity, and procession from the Apostles, the sure mark and vehicle of the Church's unity. *Episcopatus Unus* is the Apostolic foundation of the Church as one.

This would seem to complete the advance of Episcopacy to Apostolate; as *foundation*, the Episcopate is at the place in the Church which the New Testament appoints to Apostolate (Eph. 2: 20: "built on the foundation of the Apostles"). Thus we appear to have reached the identity of Apostolate-Episcopate, the formal mark of the doctrine we are studying as given at the outset of the study (for example, by Lacey: "The Apostolic foundation is permanent . . . Then where do we find it now? We answer, it is identical with the Episcopate").[1] The bishops, succeeding to the Apostles, are the possessors of that supernal authority and grace with which in the persons of the Apostles Christ first endowed His Church, and which is necessary to the fulness of her being and life.

Protestants are not cordial to this construction of the evolution and meaning of the Episcopal Ministry. They stand rather in the wake of Calvin who took the props from under Episcopal Succession in grounding the continuity of the Church in the Gospel without help from an Order. "The care is," he writes, ". . . for perpetuity of doctrine; in this the succession consists."[2] Calvin is the authority for the belief common among his followers (endorsed, however, by Lightfoot and many non-Calvinists) that 'bishop' and 'presbyter' in the New Testament are interchangeable: "In giving the name of bishops, presbyters, and pastors indiscriminately to those who govern Churches, I have done it on the authority of Scripture, which uses the words as

[1] *supra*, pp. 13, 14.
[2] *Tracts of the Reformation.*

70

synonymous."[1] None would make an issue of Calvin's dependence on Scripture; but we have gleaned in this chapter much that bears on the early Ministry from post-canonical writings with which Calvin was not familiar. *I Clement* was not known to the modern Church before 1633 (Calvin died in 1564); the *Epistles of Ignatius* were extant in a Latin version in the middle ages, but the first edition of the Greek text appeared only in 1646; the *Didache* was not known until the latter half of the nineteenth century; the same is true of the *Didascalia Apostolorum*; the *Apostolic Tradition* of Hippolytus became known in the twentieth century. Knowledge of these works could modify the position reached from studying the Scriptures only, since some of them are almost contemporary with the latest New Testament books or close enough to the New Testament to throw light back upon it. They can assist our understanding of tendencies within the New Testament insofar as what they reveal of their issue yields a clue to their real character, especially where the tendencies were too nascent in the New Testament for their direction to be certain.

Perhaps Calvin's view of the Ministry would not have been very different had he possessed these documents. Yet our findings from them seem to point to this: taking the New Testament and these subsequent records in one, doctrine and office, in primitive and early Christian history, do not appear—as Calvin's words picture it—as alternates for the Church's 'care'; there is care for both, for the Word but also for the Ministry; and it is one care, whether in Paul, the Pastoral Epistles or Irenaeus: not the Ministry *versus* the Word, but for the maintenance and purity of it.

On the whole, if we join to New Testament Church development that which in the post-Testamental epoch is the proper continuation of it, there seems good ground for holding that the major trend of Ministry in the first years of the Church is the one which, originating in the primitive Apostles, proceeds through other Apostles or their delegates to definitive historical establishment in the Episcopate,

[1] *Institutes,* IV, iii, 8.

71

when the latter has evolved from being a presiding collegium of the local Church to being the Church's superior and more general directing and teaching Order. It avails nothing against this that the Apostles in the New Testament are not called bishops, nor that the New Testament bishops are local Church ministers.

Evangelicals have been too prone because of these facts to dismiss forthwith the notion that bishops along the Church's course are the Apostles' liturgical heirs. For there was in the New Testament the wider Ministry of the Apostles as well as the local ministries; and the question comes: who did succeed to it? It is there to be assumed in its permanent phases (distinct from the peculiar relation of the Apostles as eye-witnesses of the Resurrection) after the Apostles are gone. When the bishop's position has so changed that the Apostles' functions of general responsibility and suzerainty now fall to him, who so appropriately as he could be accounted as being in the Apostles' place? The issue is not closed beforehand by identity of names. The later bishop may in the way we tried to trace have come in line *from* the New Testament bishop whose sphere of ministry was the particular Christian community; but the office and duty he has come *to* so closely correspond to those of the Apostles that effectually the mantle of the Apostles has fallen to him, and from now the bishop's New Testament prototype is ἀπόστολος rather than ἐπίσκοπος.

If the Apostles were to have successors, if Christ did intend a continuing Apostolic Ministry, as seems implied in the necessity to the Church and her work of the commission He gave to the Apostles, then Episcopacy through its development and the character it acquired became *ipso facto* the Successor in the manner spiritually valid for the Church. By the logic of historical-spiritual fact, or through the guiding hand of the Spirit, Episcopacy acceded—was made ready to accede—to Apostolate when those who were first called Apostles and their immediate deputies had passed from the scene. With the passage of the years, the place of Episcopacy as mediating the Apostles' Word and continuing their authority grew ever firmer, and it has come down to us as the main fabric of Ministry: the Historic Episcopate of the Lambeth Appeal and Quadrilateral, there named with Scripture, the Creeds and the Gospel Sacraments as requisite to any plan for Christian Reunion that seeks Anglican accord.[1]

Dr. Kirk and others describe Episcopacy as thus arising and gaining Catholic acknowledgment, as the Church's essential Ministry. "The Church of England has retained the scriptural and apostolic doctrine of the essential ministry; it has also retained the essential ministry itself by transmission from the Apostles."[2] Reformed Christendom has protested a belief that makes one Ministry of higher necessity or rank than another; it has espoused "parity of presbyters" or Ministers. This seems on secure ground so long as bishops and presbyters (priests) in the New Testament are held to be identical and one feels warranted in transferring this fact to bishops and priests (and other ministerial Orders) as now in the Church. But the picture changes if we bring to mind again the other New Testament ministries and their historical sequel, especially the ministry of the Apostles. Paul's "Am I not an Apostle?" (I Cor. 9: 1) hardly comports with parity, implying as it does something special about Apostleship to which Paul himself makes claim. Assume from their common name that later bishops directly parallel the New Testament bishops, and parity is feasible. But if Christ meant for perpetuity the special Apostolic Ministry, and if bishops whatever their original pattern of office were by the event the inheritors of it—and we have been reading the early history of the Ministry to just this issue—then parity succumbs to duality, first in the New Testament dual order of Apostles and presbyters (or presbyter-bishops), then later and in historical lineage from these, bishops and presbyters as two ministries, with primacy of the first.

The two Orders in the New Testament are familiar to

[1] *Report of the Lambeth Conference, 1920: An Appeal to all Christian People.*
[2] *The Apostolic Ministry*, p. 46.

readers of the Acts of the Apostles as "the Apostles and Elders" (Acts 15: 2, 6, 22, 23). So far our review of the formation of the Ministry has taken account chiefly of the Episcopate, with reference to Presbyterate or the ministry of Elders when the lines of Episcopacy seemed to cross into it. But Presbytery is a ministry made to its own form, whether its historical sequent be the Catholic Priesthood or the Protestant Eldership; and we must turn now in further outlining of the early Ministry to some direct consideration of it.

In an earlier section, we mentioned the Mosaic Eldership of Seventy in Numbers 11 as a moment of the tradition lying behind the Lucan story of the Seventy commissioned and sent out by Jesus. Note was taken of the widely held opinion that the Seventy of Luke signalize Christianity's mission to the Gentiles as Christ's ordaining of the Twelve was His call to Israel. This then pointed on to Luke's other work, the Acts of the Apostles, in which he narrates the Gentile mission.

It is significant in view of this that *Acts* is our source for the early Christian Eldership. Apostles and Elders, we have just noticed, greet us there as the two ministries of the Apostolic Church. At first there is no apparent relation of this primitive Christian Eldership and the Mosaic Seventy Elders. The precedent the Church is following is the contemporary Jewish Eldership. There are signs, however, that this Jewish Eldership took its model from the Mosaic order. The Eldership was traditional in Jewish life as was also the use of the number Seventy, after Moses' example (Ex. 24: 1; Num. 11: 16). Ezek. 8: 11 mentions 'seventy ancients' who appeared in the prophet's vision. The Greek translation of the Hebrew Scriptures was the Septuagint (LXX), the work of Seventy translators. Especially to be noted is the Great Council (Sanhedrin) composed of Seventy-One members, answering to the Seventy of Moses with inclusion of Moses himself. The 'Seventy' rule, both as to its prevalence and connection with 'elders,' is further evidenced in Josephus who as governor of Galilee "chose out seventy of the most prudent men, and those

74

elders in age, and appointed them to be rulers of all Galilee."[1]

Besides the Great Council there were local Councils (Mt. 5: 22; 10; 17; Mk. 13: 9), with local elders as their members. It was common to have not Seventy but Seven local elders in each community. Josephus represents Moses as decreeing: "Let there be Seven men to judge in every city, and these such as have been before most zealous in the exercise of virtue and righteousness."[2] Josephus himself, choosing Seventy as just noticed for the wider authority, chose Seven judges in every city "to hear the lesser quarrels."[3]

Allusion was made above to the absence of any readily seen connection between the early Christian Eldership and the Seventy appointed by Moses. But in one narrative in Acts we do have, not the number Seventy, but what we have just seen as its local correspondent, the number Seven. This narrative is in Acts 6: 1-6:

> And in those days, when the number of the disciples was multiplied, there arose a murmuring of the Grecians against the Hebrews, because their widows were neglected in the daily ministration.
> Then the twelve called the multitude of the disciples unto them, and said, It is not reason that we should leave the word of God, and serve tables.
> Wherefore, brethren, look ye out among you seven men of honest report, full of the Holy Ghost and wisdom, whom we may appoint over this business.
> But we will give ourselves continually to prayer, and to the ministry of the word.
> And the saying pleased the whole multitude; and they chose Stephen . . .
> Whom they set before the apostles: and when they had prayed, they laid their hands on them.

It has long been believed that these verses record the beginning not of the Eldership, but of the order of Deacons.

[1] *Wars of the Jews*, II, xx, 5.
[2] *Antiquities of the Jews*, IV, viii, 14.
[3] *Wars of the Jews*, II, xx, 5.

This belief is as old as Cyprian, though it owes to its adoption by Hooker much of its weight and prominence in modern and contemporary ecclesiastical thought. Hooker writes:

> To the degrees of ministers appointed by our Lord, His Apostles soon after annexed deacons . . . The multitude of Christians increasing in Jerusalem and waxing great, it was too much for the Apostles to teach and to minister unto tables also. The former was not to be slacked that the latter might be followed. Therefore unto this they appointed others . . . seven deacons.[1]

This identifying of the Seven with the first members of the Diaconate has its countenance from the verb διακονέω ('to serve': Acts 6: 2), the Greek source of our word 'deacon'. The Seven are to 'serve' tables, to assume the eleemosynary 'ministration' (v.1). But the corresponding noun, διακονία, is used by the Apostles of their own office, the 'service', ministry, of the Word (v. 4). Thus the force of the term seems general, not special to one division of 'service' with the thought of its becoming a technical idiom for a ministerial Order. This passage does distinguish the Seven and their Ministry from the Apostles and theirs; but διακονέω (cognate to διακόνος, deacon) is not significant of this distinction but rather, by what has just been said, answers to what is common to the Seven and the Apostles. As terms are applied, the Apostles are deacons as truly as the Seven; there is a deaconship of the Word (v.4) as the deaconship of tables (v. 1).

Moreover, other reasons exist for doubting whether the Seven mark the institution of the Diaconate. In no place in the New Testament are the Seven called deacons, nor apart from this text itself are diaconal functions, in any special view of them which emerged in the Church, ever attributed to them. In Acts 21: 8, Philip " one of the seven " is also "Philip the evangelist," a name which the record of his work in Acts 8 clearly makes appropriate. Stephen is first of the Seven as the list is given in Acts 6: 5; but he was soon

[1] *op. cit.*, V.

to testify and endure as minister of the Word, as steadfastly as any Apostle. When deacons, servants of the Church so named, do appear, in Phil. 1: 1 and in the Pastoral Epistles (I Tim. 3), they seem to be fulfilling other offices than would devolve from the service of benevolence of Acts 6: 1. On the whole, taking these considerations together, if we do not say with Farrar that the supposition that Luke regards the Seven as the first deacons is "a very old error,"[1] we can deem this supposition extremely problematic and suited to throw little light on the emergence of forms of Ministry in the Apostolic Church.

What some regard as a more likely understanding of Acts 6: 1-6 is gained through relating it, not to the Diaconate, but to the Eldership; doing this first by establishing its affinity with the account of the Mosaic-Jewish Eldership in Numbers 11. If this can be upheld, it supplies what above seemed to us wanting, a plain link of the New Testament Eldership with the Seventy of the Numbers narrative.

What, then, is the case for bringing together Acts 6: 1-6 and Num. 11: 4-17? It lies in the substantial correspondences when the passages are compared. First, the 'mixt multitude' of Num. 11: 4, distinct from Israel as is implied by "the children of Israel also" (cf. again Ex. 12: 38), is kindred to the 'multitude' of the disciples of Acts 6: 2, 5 which is similarly 'mixt' in comprising 'Grecians' (Hellenists) as well as 'Hebrews' (v. 1). Next, in both texts there is complaining by the non-Hebraic elements over material lack. In Numbers the 'mixt' ones "fell a lusting", remembering the good fare they enjoyed in Egypt (vv. 4, 5). In Acts the Grecians murmur because their needy are 'neglected' in the daily dispensing of aid (v. 1). Further again, the Seventy (Elders) in Numbers are to relieve Moses as in Acts the Seven relieve the Apostles. The Seventy "shall bear the burden with thee, that thou bear it not thyself alone" (v. 17). The Seven are appointed to the tables that the Apostles carry not all the offices alone, but are freed for

[1] *The Apostolic Ministry*, III: *The Ministry in the New Testament*, p. 138.

"the ministry of the Word" (v. 4). Not least is this resemblance: the Spirit is given to the Seventy (v. 17); the Seven are men "filled with the Holy Spirit" (v. 3).

So the two accounts seem of a pattern; and the Seventy of Numbers being Elders (11 : 16), the connecting of the Seven of Acts with the Eldership rather than with the order of Deacons so far has support. But we have had before us another parallel to the Seventy of Numbers in the Seventy of Lk. 10: 1. This parallel when we were noting it earlier[1] seemed to complete the typology: the Twelve Princes and Seventy Elders of Num. 1 and 11; the Twelve Apostles and the Seventy in the Gospels (Lk. 9: 1 and 10: 1). But typology is not the clue to the parallels Num. 11 : 16, Lk. 10: 1, Acts 6: 1-6, as we are now meeting them; rather is this to be sought in the tradition of the Lucan Seventy as symbolizing Christianity's mission to the Gentiles (as the Twelve its fulfilment of the hope of Israel). For it is conformably to this tradition that the 'Seventy' of Lk. 10 points to both the others, to the Seventy of the Mosaic economy and to the Seven of Acts 6, since what is purposed in both is not for Israel in its special demarcation, but for the 'mixt multitude' in the one, the 'Grecians' in the other. Of the relation of the Seven to this broader outlook we may see further token in the way the fury of exclusive Jewry was unleashed against the Seven, or against the first of them, the Hellenist Stephen, even more than against the Apostles (Acts 6: 9 – 8: 1).

The clue afforded, then, by the Seventy episode of Lk. 10 would seem to be this: while this episode remains of itself, in lieu of being literal history, a symbol or figuration of God's design in Christianity as reaching beyond Israel, it now appears as by this very symbolism reflecting very real history through its linkage of principle—the principle being this alertness to Christianity's farther outreach—with the account of the Seven in Acts 6 which we can receive as founded in the historical. The history which the 'Seventy' of Luke in unison with the 'Seven' of Acts thus reflects would lie, in part, by the affinities we have remarked both

[1] *supra*, p. 49.

in the 'Seven' and the 'Seventy' with the tradition of Eldership, in the establishment very early in the Church of the Eldership as an Order of Christian Ministry. This historical fact itself, make what we will of these textual connections, is momentous for our study: as well as the Apostolate, there arose in the age of the Apostles a second Ministry, the Presbyterate, born of the Holy Spirit's working within the infant Church, even if we cannot place its origin (as confidently as we do that of the Apostolate) in an act of Jesus Himself. Both Ministries wear the stamp of Old Testament precursors; the Presbyterate, our concern just now, that of the Jewish Eldership as Jewish Christians knew it contemporaneously and as reaching back, granting our above reasoning, to the primal Mosaic statute of Eldership.

This derivation of the early Christian Ministry wholly coheres with our assertion at the start that for Jesus and His followers the Church that sprang from Him was the new and true Israel ordained to carry to their issue God's ways in the old. But our inquiry has now brought to view a fact of even greater consequence: these Christian Ministries, Apostleship and Eldership, did not receive their *all* from their Jewish ancestry; their maturing character has disclosed to us other signs. We have associated with the second of them certain New Testament texts that give hints of the Church's vision as stretching past historical and race particularism to glimpse God's world intention; this association is strengthened when we note the growth of the Eldership as a Gentile Ministry, and the ordination of Elders "in every Church" by Apostles and others who minister to the Gentiles (Acts 14: 14, 23; Titus 1: 5). Is it fanciful to generalize from this and to see *in the whole early course and evolution of the Ministry by which it gains the form it will have through history, the reflex and exponent of the Church's widening vista as, taught by the Spirit and the advance of events, she learns the secret of herself and the fulness of her mission in growingly comprehending what lies hidden in the divine act and gift which called her forth?*

79

It is no necessity of our position to labour the connection of Acts 6: 1-6 with the Eldership rather than the Diaconate; nor are we suggesting that the Apostles in laying hands on the Seven were consciously creating a new ministerial Order. They may have been naming a committee to help them while they were over-burdened. But if the story of the Seven contains or implies more than this, there may be reason for regarding it as, in our word, 'reflecting' what according to the narrative of Acts did occur whatever the exact process, the addition to the Apostles of the ministry of Elders as in the story the Seven were added. We have likened the Seven to the Mosaic Seventy Elders, not because Seventy is a multiple of Seven, but in view of our comparison of Acts 6 and Num. 11 and of the way numerals were disposed in the Jewish economy. Seventy we noticed was the number for the General Council of Elders, Seven its favoured counterpart for local administration and adjudication. Local or synagogue Elders were frequently to that number. 'Seven' in Acts 6, therefore, appears a proper symbol for the Christian Eldership when we recall that, after whatever first phases, this Eldership soon tended to regular form as a local Ministry ("elders in every city": Acts 14: 23; Titus 1: 5; Acts 20: 17; cf. Josephus: "seven men to judge in every city").[1]

One could contend to the contrary of all this that the office of the Seven, to direct distribution to those in need, was very far both from the range of duty that fell to the Jewish Elder and from the spiritual and pastoral responsibility that from an early period lay upon Christian Elders (Acts 20: 17, 28; Titus 1: 5-9; I Peter 5: 1ff.; 2 and 3 John). To which may be replied: Christian Elders did have cognizance of 'welfare' in the Churches; it was to them the relief for the brethren was sent (Acts 11: 29, 30). On the other hand, the Seven or the leaders among them, 'serving tables' at the first, are not long confined to this 'service' but assume as we have seen the spiritual tasks of preaching and evangelism.

There are many references in the Book of Acts that

[1] *supra*, p. 75.

enforce the fact of the Eldership in the Apostolic Church in keeping with our argument. Before the appointment of the Seven we find no mention either of Elders or Deacons as special Ministries. There is one Ministry, that of the Word (Lk. 1: 2; Acts 6: 4), one Order of Ministers, the Apostolate, with the body of believers or 'brethren' gathered about it (Acts 2: 42; 6: 3). The Church comprises 'Apostles and Brethren' (11: 1). Following the setting apart of the Seven, we still hear nothing of Deacons, but Elders soon appear and in high place (11: 30). 'Apostles and Brethren' gives place to 'Apostles and Elders' (15: 2, 6), with the Church or 'brethren' now in fellowship with these (vv. 22, 23). Apostles and Elders seem Orders of Ministers with authority. The issue over the circumcision of Gentile believers is laid before them by a deputation to Jerusalem led by Paul and Barnabas (v. 2); the Apostles and Elders convene to examine the matter (v. 6); when decision is reached and communicated it is under their hand as leading the Spirit-guided Church (vv. 22, 23).

These and other developments move swiftly toward making Elders regular in the Church's order. Paul and Barnabas, as we have noted, ordain them in every Church (14: 23); that this practice continued we have sure sign from Titus 1: 5. Our conclusion then is—and it is the sum of our interest in relating Acts 6: 1-6 and the early Ministry —that in the formation of the Ministry it is the Eldership, not the Order of Deacons, that came next after the Apostles, and whose beginning was synchronous if not symbolically linked with the institution of the Seven. Of primary interest too to our inquiry is this: Elders were not only first in sequence to the Apostles, but were set apart of the will of the Church under act and seal of the Apostles. The Seven were chosen by the Church at the instance of the Apostles, and it was the Apostles who then laid hands upon them (Acts 6: 3, 5, 6). Paul and Barnabas are named Apostles earlier in the chapter (14: 14) that tells of their ordaining of Elders. Thus the relation of Elders (Ministers) to Church and Apostles seems to have comprised initially the two strands that were marked for permanency with the growth of Catholic Order: ordination by Apostles (bishops) but with the consent and prayers of the Church.

The Church received the Apostolate and the Eldership as Orders of Ministry; and the tradition of them retained their origin, not only in trends of order in the New Testament, but in the Jewish theocracy including the specific aspects we have studied. The Apostolate (Episcopate) was carried back to the Princes of Numbers 1, the Presbyterate (Priesthood) to the Eldership of Numbers 11. These relations were embodied in the *Ordinal* for the setting apart of Ministers, as it grew in the Church.

The Ordinal Prayers of Hippolytus' *Apostolic Tradition* are an illustration. The *Prayer for the Consecration of a Bishop* has already been noticed.[1] It contains the reference to Jewish institutions in the words: "O God . . . who didst foreordain the race of the righteous from Abraham, instituting princes and priests . . ." In the *Prayer for the Ordination of a Presbyter* the mention of the Jewish (Mosaic) precedent is more particular. The *Prayer* reads:

O God and Father of our Lord Jesus Christ . . .
Look upon this Thy servant and impart to him the spirit of grace and counsel, that he may share in the presbyterate and govern Thy people with a pure heart.
As Thou didst look upon the people of Thy choice and didst command Moses to choose presbyters whom Thou didst fill with the spirit which Thou hadst granted to Thy minister . . . So now, O Lord, grant that there may be preserved among us unceasingly the Spirit of Thy grace, and make us worthy that in faith we may minister to Thee praising Thee in singleness of heart . . .[2]

The Roman Catholic *Ordinal* similarly recounts the Mosaic appointments of the Book of Numbers, in conformity with the Church's general belief in the continuity

---

[1] *supra*, p. 69.
[2] *The Apostolic Tradition* (ed. Gregory Dix), pp. 4, 5; 13, 14.

of Catholic Orders and the Old Testament priesthood. Here are its words:

> Truly it is meet and right, fitting and health-giving, that we should at all times and in all places give thanks unto Thee, O Lord, holy, Father Almighty, everlasting God, source of all honours and dispenser of all dignities . . . Whence also there came into being priestly orders and levitical offices appointed for spiritual mysteries, so that when Thou hadst set over the people high priests as their rulers, Thou mightest choose men of a second order and in a lower status to be partners with them in their society and work. In such wise didst Thou extend the spirit of Moses to the minds of seventy prudent men in the wilderness, that using them as helpers among the people he might govern with competence innumerable multitudes.

We have devoted this chapter to data from early Christianity that are widely regarded as basic to the argument for Apostolic Episcopal Succession. What those who so consider them derive from them, put into a few sentences, would come to this:

The New Testament Ministries of Apostles and Elders, cornerstone of the Church's historic Ministry of Bishops and Presbyters (Priests), did not arise—and were not in the main course of the Church's thought believed to have arisen —as a historical chance or a human invention. Their connection with the prior Jewish order, held by Jesus as proleptic of His own purpose, their emergence in the New Testament through the activity of Jesus and of the Church directed by His Spirit, all mark them as being of the will of God and of Christ's coming to the world to establish that will. These two Ministries not only testify to the way Jesus and the first Christian believers knew the Church born of Him to be heir to Israel's hope as it had been engendered of the activity of God in her history; these Ministries are themselves entwined about these historical roots and partake of the substance and character of God's historical self-manifestation whence Christianity was begotten. They did not come into being from expediency or merely because

83

the Church deemed advantageous such provision for ordering her life as she had by them; they were God's choice for the Church, and with the Church they were God's benefaction to men in His new covenanting with them.

There were other Ministries in the New Testament than the two to which chiefly we have been giving our thought. In particular, the *deacons* as servants of the Church and attendants of bishops and presbyters became a definitive third Order. On the first stages of the diaconate students of the New Testament are not of one mind, quite apart from the variant understandings of Acts 6: 1-6. But before the New Testament period closes deacons are a definite Ministry collateral to bishops and elders in the local community (Phil. 1: 1; I Tim. 3). Ignatius, as we have seen,[1] will soon associate them with bishops and presbyters as co-integral to the Church's life. Thus the threefold Order is reached, to become for much of the Church throughout her history the norm for the Ministry. Justin Martyr speaks of those "whom we call deacons" as distributing the bread and wine at the Sacrament and carrying away a portion for those who are absent.[2] Apostles and Elders, however, are primary and paramount in our study of the formative phase of the Ministry as a foundation for doctrine. They were Ministers of the parent Church at Jerusalem, where as we saw they speak already with authoritative voice (Acts 15: 2, 6, 22, 23). In their place in the Church and in the way the Church looks to them, they are progenitor-types of the great Catholic episcopal and priestly Orders of Ministry.

We have completed two parts of our task: the outlining of the doctrine of Apostolic Episcopal Succession; the collating of the data and evidence adducible from Scripture and early Christian history in support of this doctrine. We now turn to attempt some appraisal of the doctrine and the

[1] *To the Trallians*, cited *supra*, p. 61.
[2] *First Apology*, I, 62.

argument for it. This will lead on finally to our own statement of the Doctrine of the Ministry, in the form that seems most consonant with the facts and principles pertaining to the Ministry which our inquiry will have brought to light.

Chapter 3

EXAMINATION OF THE DOCTRINE OF APOSTOLIC EPISCOPAL SUCCESSION

W E have already made it clear that, in our understanding, the doctrine of Apostolic Episcopal Succession is built on concern for vital Christian truths and the Church is immeasurably indebted to it for its witness to these truths. It has been a principal bearer of them far more than is realized by many who do not hold the doctrine; perchance by some who do. On the other hand, the question whether the doctrine is in some important respects vulnerable is one that can properly be raised. We shall consider in this chapter truths and aspects of Christianity which this doctrine effectually upholds, and then in further appraisal turn to ways in which it is unconvincing as ordinarily expressed.

I

Essential Truths witnessed to and emphasized by the Doctrine of Apostolic Episcopal Succession

First to note is this: This doctrine, affirming the necessity or at least the vital value of certain ministerial Orders, and the peculiar spiritual efficacy of certain sacraments administered by members of these Orders, emphatically declares Christianity to be a religion of salvation and divine saving grace. For to what end are these Orders and Ordinances necessary or efficacious? We may not wholly agree with the Tractarians who, as W. L. Knox told us earlier,[1] "pro-

---

[1] *supra*, p. 27.

claimed the sacramental system of the Catholic Church as the divinely appointed means by which man has access to God." Nor with Knox himself when he avers: "Communion between the soul and God may take the form of some external action to the proper performance of which a special promise of grace is attached. This form of communion with God is the sacramental system of the Catholic Church."[1] But agree or no, we cannot deny that the premiss in both of these is a Christianity to which access to and communion with God are basal for its message and meaning.

Catholics regard God as having provided two things: salvation in the Gospel through the redeeming and mediatorial work of Christ, and an instituted Means and Order through which men receive the salvation. He has not given the salvation and left men to embrace and appropriate as they may. To have done just this would be precarious, as Protestants also perceive when they think of God as decreeing with the salvation a Word of salvation, and as giving the Holy Spirit to help men proclaim it and to lead those who hear to saving acceptance of it. Catholics are in accord with this, but maintain as well that with the salvation and His ordinance for the preaching of it, God willed the institute of salvation to help the people for whom the salvation is ordained to proof and possession of it. What we are saying is that however we adjudge in other ways this Catholic belief, an institute of salvation in ministerial orders and sacraments does imply salvation as Christianity's being and purpose. The whole Catholic structure, not least the element closest to our interest, the Catholic doctrine of the Ministry, would be pointless without this pre-conviction.

Putting it in another form, Christianity in the Catholic rendering of it is not a moralism or ethico-cultural idealism, or a mere crusade for humanitarian reform. Perhaps the deepest division among Christians—deeper than that between Catholics and Protestants—is the one which separates those to whom Christianity is of interest chiefly as a

[1] *op. cit.*, p. 51.

quest for values or for the ideal fulfilment of life, with Jesus and His teaching as the norm for this, from those for whom Christianity is salvation or redemption not humanly attained nor even conceived, but born of God's unmerited favour and made effectual through His gracious working in men's behalf. Sacraments and Orders belong to this latter Christianity; both Catholic and Evangelical Churches are grounded upon it. Catholic Christianity has perhaps with some justice been called semi-pelagian through the way its people are taught to rely on ceremonial and penitential works. But even these works are for the sake of salvation, the soul's eternal safety; they are part of the Catholic methodology for appropriating the salvation miracle and gift. Their object is not fulfilled in fostering effort toward ideals. We may owe it more to Catholicism than to Protestantism that during the past one hundred years Christianity, assailed by the "acids of modernity", has persisted as an objective Salvation-Faith, instead of becoming an idealistically-toned ethicism valued as giving religious reinforcement to personal and social morality.

Christianity exalts the ethical and put to the proof is unmatched in its ethical power; but its coefficient even here is not religious idealism but redemptive grace. The Catholic doctrine of the Ministry clearly acknowledges and presupposes this grace in making the Ministry the medium and ministrant of it. In a similar way, in enduing the Ministry with prerogative to bind and loose, to effectuate in men the divine forgiving, it postulates the fact of divine forgiveness and the correspondent nature of man's essential need. Apostolic Succession may not be the best testament to this divine grace and forgiveness, but it does attest it, to the depth of being void of effect without the assurance of it. The assumptions of Apostolic Succession stand with Christianity being professed, not simply as a way of life, but as Redemption-Faith through its origin in God's total act of redemption in Jesus Christ. All, therefore, who adhere to this redemptive meaning of Christianity can find worth in Apostolic Succession and so far common cause with confessors of it. This "common cause" has become important

88

in a time when Christianity is finding necessary a revaluation of its belief in redemption and what it implies of man's state and the character of his hope, in face of a humanistic optimism that falsifies the more tragic aspects of the reality of man and whose ingression into Christian thinking has made it hard in some instances to distinguish Christian from secular anthropologies and philosophies of religion.

Sometimes people who are not sure of this redemptive quality and mission of Christianity, but who have embraced its ethical principles, come together in the Service of Communion, seeking through it closer unity one with another in unison with the spirit of Jesus and a fortifying of their will to be brotherly and to work for peace and brotherhood throughout the world. Sacramental worship is for such ends; it is poor if it does not lead to them. But it is not for them immediately, for human fellowship and common purpose. The Holy Supper is the sacrament of the Broken Body and Shed Blood. The theme of its celebration is not our movement toward union among ourselves but God's movement toward us in which we are drawn one to another in being first, severally and in concert, drawn to Him. The meanings of the sacrament lie deep in those reaches of the soul where God meets man to forgive and renew, to give grace for repentance and holiness. It is these ends of the sacrament, of the whole Christian Evangel, that are the import of sacraments as acts of grace and that make 'holy' the 'orders' and calling of the Christian Ministry. Once again, Apostolic Succession may not accord these realities their perfect embodiment but it is grounded upon them, upon God's saving approach to man and His act for man's salvation in Christ's self-offering. The proclamation of this divine act, the ministration to men's souls of the benefits issuing from it, a ministration falling from hand to hand down the generations, is the thread of Christian history; the heart too of Apostolic Succession.

Apostolic Succession is a signpost to God's path through the Christian centuries and to the truth and power borne along it to be for each age—for our own—freshly available.

In words cited earlier from Archbishop Frederick Temple:[1]

> The purpose of the Succession is to link the Church back to the first appointment of the Apostles by our Lord; and to make men feel the unity of the Body as it comes down the stream of history, and to touch their hearts with some sense of the Power the Lord bequeathed when He ascended on high and gave gifts to men.

This expresses great verities and vitalities of the Church's historical life, and it prompts to a highly favourable estimation of the doctrine of Apostolic Succession that its witness has established many multitudes in their trust and certainty of them.

This witness is one which in our time almost more than in any other the Church dare not forgo. For we have come to a day when these Christian actualities are impugned and challenged to the degree of being universally in jeopardy. Or where not impugned, they meet what is yet more inimical and deadly: complete neglect. " There is more open and aggressive atheism," writes the late Archbishop of York, " than at any other period of human history. ... Far more general is the attitude of complete indifference to religion and ignorance of its nature."[2] Dr. Garbett is speaking especially of England, and we are apt on this continent with the comfortable " it is not so here " when such a tale is heard. This is insubstantial solace, since Christianity's contemporary predicament, the perils overt and hidden that beset it, are a world phenomenon. Contrary faiths have multiplied against it and, what is more insidious, everywhere, not least in our Western life, Christianity is contested by or confused with a social and cultural pattern of wellbeing that millions find too alluring to pause to ask, Is it Christian? Does it promise the distinctive Christian fulfilments?

These manifestations are prevalent enough to prompt J. V. L. Casserley to write under the title *The Retreat from*

[1] *supra*, p. 25.
[2] *In an Age of Revolution*, pp. 53, 54.

Christianity in the Modern World; and it falls in with what we have just said that he expresses the 'Retreat' as twofold, not only into irreligion, but more especially now into religion. His words are these:

> The distinguishing characteristic of the last two hundred and fifty years, is the extent to which many . . . have attempted to erect and live in the shadow of systems of total irreligion. But this period is drawing to a close, the retreat from Christianity into some alternative form of religion is the more profoundly and enduringly important form of the retreat from Christianity. The retreat from Christianity into irreligion does no more than create a spiritual vacuum, but the retreat from Christianity into religion may do something more terrible . . . it may fill that vacuum with reborn superstitions and mythologies, giving new life to the paganisms and idolatries from which the Gospel once delivered us, and may now have to deliver us all over again.[1]

If this is a true picture; if new irruptions into the religious scene and the sophisticated tempering of our Christianity to the "graven images" our civilization makes unto itself are bringing it about that, in place of "the evangelization of the world in this generation"—the watchword of what seems only yesterday—the Gospel must in many ways start again at the bottom and recover ground it once held; then nothing can save or serve us but to hear and have the Gospel in its stark incidence upon our life and ways and in its full character as the Gospel of God, with the notes that are its own of judgment and repentance and grace abounding to all. We are saying here that the Catholic doctrine of the Ministry is, by its integral assumptions, inextricably bound to this Gospel. To affirm sacramental mediation of sovereign grace, to stand in the assurance that God has appointed an order and channel whereby this grace unveiled in Christ can reach to those for whom it is designed, does bespeak prior conviction of sovereign grace and hold in allegiance to the Gospel ordained to bear it. This, then, is our first commendation

[1] p. 5.

of the doctrine of Apostolic Episcopal Succession: its dependence on the New Testament Word and *raison d'être* in the Truth which, in association with this doctrine or not, the Church to be the Church must have; and its having kept the sign of this Truth in years when its finality has lain in eclipse and there has been much trembling of the pillars of confidence in it.

A second great service of Apostolic Episcopal Succession is the way it has confessedly upheld and fostered the unity of the Church, both in faith and life. Apostolic Succession has symbolized the integrity of the Church's teaching and has helped to preserve this integrity as the teaching has been transmitted from age to age. Practically in respect of her unity the Church has failed; a divided Christendom is one of the big facts of present Christian existence, however we evaluate it or assign its causes. But Apostolic Succession is predicated upon this unity; there is one Apostolate. The testimony Apostolic Episcopal Succession has given to unity and continuity, both of the Church and the Gospel, is seen not without reason as auguring for it a substantial if not necessary part in the recovery of them.

It will be recalled that in the second century when bewilderment because of contradictory Gospels was pushing the Church down the scale to impotence and disintegration. Irenaeus and others turned for assurance and guidance to the men standing in mid-stream from those to whom the Gospel Word originally came. Where if not there could be had the teaching authoritative and normative for the whole Body?

If authority and norm were desired then, what of our need now? It would be hard to picture more diversity and indirection than the Church now exhibits, not over ways of expressing Christianity but regarding what Christianity or the Gospel is. The Church is a scene of radical disunity not just formally or organizationally, but in the ways of understanding her essential belief and purpose. The World Council of Churches and its Assemblies are a great fact of our time; they are alive to this disunity and are seeking what may lead to melioration of it. But they are also bringing this disunity to focus through—rightly—counting it a move forward to reach clarification of it by the method whereby each Church places its special professions and the reasons for them before the others. This is a first step toward healing breaches that for the moment accents the breaches. The Evanston World Council Assembly, 1954, will live in history to the Church's honour through the candour and spirit of charity in which differences were stated and examined; but just by this, it was a register of differences. Christians found themselves apart on the main theme of the Assembly, the Christian Hope for the world; they had no sure common certainty of the relation of Hope and Faith.

Evanston, moreover, was only a partial index of world Christian divergence. While it was in session the head of the largest Christian Communion made it the occasion for reiterating that Communion's inveterate demand, as the one means to the reunion of Christendom, that the other Churches conform to it and accept its hierarchy and doctrine, much of which is anathema to millions in those Churches and is likely so to remain. Certain other Churches, some even among those gathered at Evanston, are hardly less exclusive. The Patriarch of the Orthodox Church in the United States declares unashamedly:

> As a member and priest of the Orthodox Church I believe that the Church in which I was baptized is in very truth the Church, i.e. the true Church and the only true Church. I believe that for many reasons: by personal conviction and by the inner testimony of the Spirit which breathes in the sacraments of the Church and by all that I could learn from Scripture and from the universal tradition of the Church. I am compelled therefore to regard all other Christian Churches as deficient . . . Christian reunion for me is just universal conversion to Orthodoxy.[1]

Genuine conviction such as animates these words is to be

[1] See Georges Florovsky, in Baillie and Marsh, *Intercommunion*, pp. 203, 204.

honoured, in Roman and Greek Church leaders or wherever it is encountered; yet who can contemplate these attitudes of the great historic Churches without feeling how hard a path leads to Church reunification, how humanly unhealable are the rifts and rents in the fabric of the Universal Church?

But in our context this is not the worst. For we are thinking of basically conflicting renderings of the Gospel such as made Irenaeus listen for an authentic voice in the Episcopal heirs of the Apostles; and it is not conflicts of this sort that have sundered the great Churches, for all that we have seen of the unyielding strain in their separation. On the centralities of Christian truth and belief the Churches, East, West and Reformed, are in credal accord. All confess the Triune Deity, the Lordship and Saviourhood of Jesus Christ, the divine Agency for salvation of the Holy Spirit; all believe in God's gift of sanctification and the hope of eternal life. We must look elsewhere than to the lines that mark off Orthodox, Catholic and Protestant for the causes of the prevailing confusion over the nature of the Gospel and of the general weakening of ardour for its assumptions and claims.

They are found, not where one major segment of Christendom meets another, but in the vagueness and hesitancy in all the Churches concerning Christianity's essential being. There are liberalist and traditionalist versions of it, with a profuse miscellany under each head, that make it almost two religions or a medley of them. Views of Jesus range all the way from esteeming Him a good man whose example is before us to emulate, to notions of His Deity incongruous with His being a man at all; from humanitarian dogmas of His person to docetic ascription to Him of omniscience and infallibility. Salvation—the end offered in Christianity—is to some the gaining of a guarantee of heaven in the after life along with escape from a literal hell; to others training in character or present aspiration after purposeful living, with 'reward' here and now in unity within oneself and mutually enriching outward and common relations; still others take from both these con-

94

ceptions and offer modulations and blendings of them that are again too numerous to name. Preachers amid the welter are a law to themselves; each presents the Christian theme as his own understanding, or predilection, instructs or impels. Sects and parties multiply, giving the notes of the Evangel all varieties of proportional importance: now this belief, now that, minor in other presentations or omitted from them, is lifted to the essentials or absolutized into being almost the whole. To outsiders as to many within the tokens of a common faith among Christians are hard to discern. In consequence, multitudes doubt if there is such a faith; multitudes more are distracted in their search for it.

This despair of a faith is without question a *malaise* of our time. Many today find nothing in the world of such worth as constrains them to live for it supremely; nothing to draw their diverse interests together into a total meaning and compelling purpose. Such persons have lost or have never seen the vision of what life is for; they are lost souls through having missed their way. On the manner of the 'conversion' that would 'save' them, none of us is clear.

We are not suggesting that this pathetic and unhopeful mood now so familiar is due solely to divisions within Christianity or to the mental unsettlement arising from the multiplicity of interpretations of it. Events have had a share: wars and subsequent disillusionment plus other crises, with present fears because much worse disasters are now among things possible. These two influences are not unconnected; world calamities have made easy a chaos of opinion and emotion over the reality of God and His purpose for a world in which the things that the past two generations have witnessed can occur. On the other hand, we have already alluded to the fateful changes in the secular and social outlook for which this breakdown of faith in God has opened the door, the new idolatries so unashamed and eager that the true gods seem in the 'twilight' and listless by the side of them. Many people claim to have in these other 'faiths' the very thing we have just said vast multitudes lack: the means to purposeful and socially creative existence.

95

These, then, are some of the conditions that lend gravity to Christianity's present dilemma; they are of the character, moreover, implied by our suggestion that this dilemma shows parallels to the one faced by Irenaeus. Now, as then, other gospels ravage the field and there is perplexity over the substance of the One Gospel and over how its truth can be ascertained. Our time, as did that earlier one, calls from the depth for a Word spoken to and heard above our conflicts, our anxious and enfeebling indecision, renewing and reinvigorating the Church's own persuasion of Christianity's once-for-all sufficiency and re-authenticating its message as one for all mankind.

In the former instance this Word was sought in the Episcopate holding the seal of the Apostles. We are saying in this second note of our appraisal that Apostolic Episcopacy has signalized this One Word throughout the Church's course, in being a continuing Ministry. Should the Church, then, in its present need for the Word, turn its ear to it?

We can hear an answer reminding us that in one all-essential regard the Church's case today is *not* parallel to that of the early patristic age. Then—as we have stressed—there was no canonical New Testament. Now not only does the Church possess it, but the New Testament is generally received in its witness to the Word and as the standard for Christian faith and life.

This is so, and our present knowledge of Christianity mostly hangs on the New Testament unfolding of it. Yet it is not apparent that men are thereby guided to common conviction concerning Christianity and its essential teaching. Almost the opposite is the case; the most divided Christians are those with the Bible in their hands. Interpretations of the Bible are multifarious, and every one of a vast array of warring sects will invoke it in its support. "Searching" the Bible to the rule of individual inclination or "private interpretation," so far from restoring the disrupted Christian household to "the unity of the faith," has been an agent of still further disruption especially of evangelical Christendom. We can hardly hope in view of this that pointing to the Bible will of itself produce and establish the coherence we have seen as wanting in the Church's approach and appeal to our age. The Bible is where the Word is to be had, but history does not encourage the confidence that the Bible alone, if the people have no other guidance, will ensure or of necessity even assist general Christian accord.

It is not that we would have Christian thinking all out of one mould, or what is gained from the Bible understood and presented in one uniform way. Certainly we are not asking for some ecclesiastical official interpreter of Scripture. Let there be freedom with the diversity that properly attends it. No one person or group has all the insight nor encircles the light that breaks from the Sacred Word. Yet granting this, there is one Christianity that exists as itself, not a thing so wholly unformed that each of us can make it to his will. It is of the one God and of *His* will, of His purpose ever one with His nature and will. It is in its integral unity one Faith and Doctrine, however articulate in the speech and thought idiom of many ages and peoples. "We need a word," writes Sanday, "to express a deep centrality of thought"[1] down the Church's course, the path through history of the Christian mind. This centrality finds proof in the persisting identity of the Christian Faith; with all the digressions, the vacillation, the room within Christianity for individual thought with its too ready declension to eccentricities of religious belief, there is historically this one ongoing constituent order of testimony and teaching. Christianity began and has continued as the one Word to be preached at all times and to all nations (Rev. 14: 6; Mk. 13: 10); so exclusively the one that an angel from heaven preaching another would be accursed (Gal. 1: 8). Apart from texts, is it not a demand of reason that Christianity as a historical movement should have constancy of character for orderliness of action and for progress in its world mission?

In the New Testament, this continuing, ordering element is the doctrine of the Apostles ("they continued steadfastly in the Apostles' doctrine": Acts 2: 42). Is this

[1] *Christology and Personality*, p. 22.

the answer always? has the Church at any time no more to
do than to lay to heart and when she speaks re-enunciate
the teaching of the Apostles as the New Testament has preserved it? Is the "deep centrality" for the whole line of
history here already marked out and complete?

Quite definitely the matter is not thus simple. The later
Church came to hold as central many beliefs that do not
occur in the preaching of the Jerusalem Apostles. C. H.
Dodd notes several of these beliefs: "Jesus is not," he
writes, "in the Jerusalem *kerygma* called 'Son of God' . . .
The *kerygma* does not assert that Christ died for our sins. . .
[nor] that the exalted Christ intercedes for us."[1] Upholders
of Apostolic Succession usually endorse the acknowledgment of the ecumenical creeds as in the Lambeth Reunion
Call where in the bishops' proposals for reunion they are
co-ordinate with the Scriptures, the Sacraments and the
Apostolic Ministry. But the creeds, even the Apostles'
Creed, contain things that were never in the mind of the
Apostles. "The Apostles' doctrine" of Acts 2: 42 would
embody Christianity only in inchoate form. The Church
has now in the substance of what she professes much that
would not have come to Peter's mind when preaching at
Pentecost and would have had scant meaning for him.

If the Church's Gospel, then, is Apostolic, this does not
mean that its contents are identical word for word with
what the Apostles knew and proclaimed. These Apostles
themselves were told there was truth they could not yet bear
(John 16: 12), and the promise to the Church through
them was of guidance *into* truth (v. 13) not in the perpetual
reduplicating of truth already given. Even the first believers
'continued' in the Apostles' doctrine; they were not fixated
in it. From the beginning in the understanding of her
message the Church is en route, movement is of her essence;
whence the beliefs Dodd does not find in the primitive
preaching are present soon after, as other parts of the New
Testament make clear. Yet with all this rule of advance, it
remains: the Church continued in the Apostles' doctrine
and "continued steadfastly". This phrase is the epitome of

[1] *The Apostolic Preaching and its Developments*, pp. 47-49.

98

Apostolicity for the whole of Christian history. The Church's Gospel stems from the Apostles' witness, is steadfastly faithful to it, but *continues* in it: in continuity with it reaches out to *ever fuller comprehension of itself* as the promised guidance into truth is given and as, with changing human needs and demands upon him, the Christian scribe brings forth from his one Treasure things new and old.

This is the Apostolic Ministry, the work of this scribe; Ministry not for the simple repeating of what the Apostles said and did, but for interpreting and applying, in each age and human conjuncture, the Christian reality: " Jesus and the Resurrection" as the Apostles first knew and named it. The Apostles did this interpreting for their own time and people; it remains for all time the Apostolic function; and what it yields 'continues' the work and faith of the Apostles, though not chained to what the Apostles or anyone grasped of Christianity in its initial years. The Apostolic function is bigger than if it were so held, more creative and prophetic. As the Word of God is not bound so neither is the Apostolic Ministry, save to the Word as were the Apostles (Acts 6: 4); to be bound *as were* the Apostles rather than *to* them is what truly defines Apostolic Ministry. This Ministry and function, holding in one this bondage to the Word and creative freedom in it, was never more needed than now when (as we have seen) the freedom has slipped from the bounds within which it served the common advance to lure religious people into so many and diverse byways that byways are taken for highways, and the comings and goings of words have all but deafened us to the One Continuing Word.

There is place, let us repeat, for religious diversity. No one, not even the most ardent Church reunionist, wants one all-inclusive monolithic Church organization, a stereotype in all its expressions. Diversities among Christians can be a mark of life when each sees in the others essential Christian existence, their differences proliferating from a common centre to serve a common end. But so many of our present differences are *ec*centric. It is not that Christians are divided, but we have no generally received standard or reference-centre for testing the divisions, to determine which of them are of the Body as against schismatic 'hivings-off' from it. In Christendom without a reference-centre, all our divisions become eccentric. This is not diversity appropriate to life but to chaos, to the negation of the Church's being as one, of its Catholicity. For Catholicity is not a name for the total body of Christians however constituted, or where the units comprised by it are left each to take its stamp from its specialties of belief; but it is *integral* wholeness ordered under Truths and Meanings that are one for all, and are those which belong formatively to Christianity's being and in which its purpose inheres.

The Church has these truths now as always in "continuing in the Apostles' doctrine," in standing steadfast on "the foundation of the Apostles" (Eph. 2 : 20). Only we have now seen that this 'continuing' means continually increasing in realization of the doctrine as well as maintaining it as formally given; and standing on the Apostles' foundation means not just keeping the Church stable on its historic base but renewing and fulfilling creatively for each age the Church's fidelity to the Apostles' Word. This is Apostolicity within the Church, and its work is plainly always to be done. Hence the necessity to the Church and her order of *perpetual Apostolate*, not just Apostles at the first. This Apostolate is the Church's Ministry, truly by this naming of its office the Apostolic Ministry. It exists for all the ends of Apostleship, for testifying to the Resurrection and proclaiming salvation in the divine Kingdom; for the renewing and building up of the 'fellowship' and for maintenance of the 'doctrine' through growing comprehension of it and vision of its fulness for the world's life. Apostolicity is to the Church the servant of her unity and increase of faith, and of her world vocation. Ministry fulfilling this service through the centuries, perpetual Apostolate as we have named it, is the true Apostolic Succession; and by the place this Ministry has had always in the Church and the Church's ever-present need for it, this Apostolic Succession is not a thing to argue for or against but is self-evidently a fact of the Church's being.

What is special about the belief we are studying is that it asks us to discern it precisely in historical Episcopal Succession. "Episcopacy," we learned before from a prominent Church of England spokesman, "is guarantee of continuity in apostolic teaching and administration."[1] Succession of ministers through episcopal ordination is held to be in respect both of Faith and Order the God-given focus of unity in the Church. This particular assertion which identifies Episcopacy with the Church's needed Ministry we have yet to adjudge; what we are now insisting on as not arguable is the need itself of a continuing Ministry for certainty and furtherance of the Church's Faith. Would not such Ministry go far to afford the reference and rallying centre for unity and purposeful endeavour in the Gospel which we have seen the Church now lacks? Some means whereby the Christian Faith in its fulness could throughout the world be heard as one, with the directness and authority of those who know whence they have received, would be of incalculable benefit against the present fragmentation and dissipation of the Church's witness and energies in a time that calls desperately for something better from the Church. Apostolic Episcopal Succession implies Ministry for just this end; its postulate is the one Apostolate undergirding the Church's oneness and having as its aim to uphold the Word and Authority derived from Christ through the Apostles and to summon men to heed them; an aim which answers item by item to what we have just said would effectually set the Church in the course to meet the demands that the world's bafflement and disorder now lay upon it.

The way the doctrine of Apostolic Episcopal Succession has been awake to these essentials for the Church is our second word in praise of it. It is still to ask whether this doctrine is necessary to the truths and aims it has fostered and attested; or could equal attestation cohere with other beliefs concerning the Ministry to which many come who approach the problem of the Ministry by other paths.

We shall name one other value of Apostolic Episcopal

[1] *supra*, p. 68.

Succession that adds further weighty cause for positive appreciation of it: the help it has given in apprehending the essential divine quality that belongs to the Church's Ministry. We have already touched on the principal aspect of this in speaking of the Ministry's *shaliach* character. When Jesus says to those whom He sends: "All power is given unto *me* . . . Go *ye*, therefore, and teach" (Mt. 28: 18, 19), the imperative escapes being a *non sequitur* only as the Divine Sender and the human sent are in effectual unity. The divine quality of the Apostles' Ministry is secured by their participation through this unity with Christ in the 'power' for Ministry God has 'given' to Him.

A conception that discloses in its inwardness this divine relation of the Ministry through the union of Christ and His Ministers is one common throughout the New Testament: the conception of witness. The witness (μάρτυς) can be the martyr strictly, the one who witnesses unto death (Acts 22: 20). But in wider reference the name is given to those who, whatever it entail, bear steadfast testimony to what they have seen and known (I Thess. 2: 10). Jesus had seen and known God whom none other had seen (John 1: 18; 17: 25). He therefore can declare God (1: 18) or be God's faithful and true witness (Rev. 3: 14); He is witness to God as of the Godhead ("in the bosom of the Father"). Another place where witness to the Divine is borne by One Himself Divine is John 15: 26: the Spirit witnesses to Christ. These are veins of a deepest whole truth in association with 'witness': *all* within the Godhead knowing the things of God (Mt. 11: 27; John 17: 25; I Cor. 2: 10) witness mutually, each naming and attesting the others (John 1: 18; Mk. 9: 7; Mt. 16: 17; Rom. 1: 4; I Cor. 12: 3).

But Jesus unites to this divine witnessing the Apostles' witness to Himself. "The Spirit shall witness to me . . . Ye also having been with me shall bear witness" (John 15: 26, 27). If another address of Jesus to the disciples, "as the Father hath sent me, even so send I you," established on His direct verbal authority the Apostles as the *shaliach* of Christ as Christ was *shaliach* of God, this present text makes them with almost equal directness the *shaliach* of the Spirit. The Spirit is 'sent' to witness (15: 26); He is given to the Apostles who also witness through the Spirit 'in' them (14: 17; 15: 26, 27). The Spirit and the Apostles are sharers in witness (Acts 5: 32) as Christ and the Apostles. This community of witness, of Christ, the Spirit and the Ministry, to the same truth and for the same end, is the soul of the divine relation of the Ministry and carries high consequence for the Ministry and for our Doctrine. For all witness is by the one power; that which enables the witness of Christ and the Holy Spirit is alone the Minister's enablement. So in the first days of the Church: Ministers as co-witnesses with the Spirit wait for the power of the Spirit (Acts 1: 8: "ye shall receive power after the Spirit is come upon you, and ye shall be my witnesses"). The power of the Spirit in the Minister is his immediately as having the Spirit, just as those whom Jesus sent forth had abiding assurance of His power in His presence with them (Mt. 28: 18-20).

No doctrine of the Ministry ever claimed, or could claim, more for the Ministry than this—which the New Testament thus affirms of it and Christ and the Holy Spirit in the fashion just seen actually bring to it. There may have been wrong formulations of the claim but not in the way of exceeding the Fact. The doctrine of Apostolic Succession or more generally the Catholic doctrine of the Ministry does as to its form spell out this height and depth of the ministerial calling. It does this in those parts of it that to Protestants seem most dubious. For the power of the keys, priestly absolution, the target of Protestant denunciation, aside from the words of Jesus that seem to bestow it (Mt. 16: 19; John 20: 23), does imply for the Ministry a divine state and quality such as we are thinking of in this section, and the authority Christ alone can grant; Paul's absolving, we recall, was "in the person of Christ" (2 Cor. 2: 10). This is not to claim validity for everything in Catholic theory of priesthood; the Catholic belief simply, as the doctrine of Apostolic Succession, lays on the Ministry responsibilities that copy formally Christ's gift and command to Ministers.

The Catholic doctrine distinguishes the Ministry by its consecration to spiritual duties; however the Ministry is of the Fellowship in which no one is above another, it has honour within it from the sacred character and necessity of the tasks for which it is set apart.

In the foregoing paragraphs we have recorded three things as upheld by the doctrine of Apostolic Episcopal Succession. They are vital to Christianity and of urgent consequence for her position and mission in the world. First, this doctrine has never ignored the primary facts of salvation as some modern renderings of Christianity have done. This is of high moment in a time when it has become freshly evident that as other than a religion of salvation, as a provision for enhancing civil and cultural excellence in place of being man's total restitution at the hand of God, Christianity does not offer what the world sorely needs; not now more than at other times—the world's need is always that of a sinful world—but the disturbed state of human affairs and the pitfalls hidden in their course make the need palpable as at few stages of man's devious and chequered way.

Then, as a second service Apostolic Succession has helped to keep the Church mindful of its roots in God's historical self-revealing action and of Christianity's self-identical character as it emerged and grew to its form in history. This too has special timeliness in view of influences now threatening Christianity with erosion save as they are met by quickened awareness of the Faith's proper integrity and zeal to maintain it on its sufficient grounds, with whatever freedom or variation of expression and interpretation befits a living enterprise. Our third appreciation of Apostolic Succession relates to the way it has shown forth the Minister as Christ's ambassador and witness, with fulness of power not his own, but the selfsame power that dwelt in Christ and is possessed by the Minister solely through Christ's gift of His Spirit to him.

These three the doctrine of Apostolic Episcopal Succession certifies to our mind by its very principles. They are not the complete case for the doctrine, more could be said in behalf of it; but its gift to Christendom has been abundant in its direct and indirect sustenance of these, when many in the Church have wavered or have had little care or thought to spare for them.

There remains, however, the question of how far the testimony it gives to these vital emphases warrants our acceptance of the doctrine of Apostolic Episcopal Succession as such or in the body of what it asserts concerning the Ministry. Or could another doctrine witness as authentically in these regards while as a whole doctrine being more agreeable to the full requirement which the just weighing of all aspects of the problem of the Ministry lays upon it? This question leads to the next stage of our undertaking.

II

Critical Reflection on the Doctrine of Apostolic Episcopal Succession

Our effort now will be to set the doctrine of Apostolic Episcopal Succession in the light of the central issues pertaining to the Ministry and to the relation of the Ministry to the Gospel and the Church. These issues have already appeared to us in what we have gleaned from Scripture and Christian history.

We may begin with the question whether the supporters of Apostolic Succession have sufficiently examined the character of history and the role of institutions within it. The analysis of Apostolic Succession may turn largely on the meaning of history, the way we understand God's working within it, and the nature of the agencies which He employs.

A basic consideration is whether history is equal or homogeneous; or is there an internal essential history conjoined within the whole with another that is circumstantial or phenomenal? Can we separate the inalienable stuff of history from what is adventitious?

Here I transcribe from Toynbee:

Is there some intelligible field of historical study which is
absolute and not merely relative to the particular social
environment of particular historians? So far, our inquiry
seems to have brought out the fact that historical thought
takes a deep impress from the dominant institutions of the
transient social environment in which the thinker happens
to live. If this impress proved to be so profound and so
persuasive as actually to constitute the *a priori* categories in
the historian's mind, that conclusion would bring our
inquiry to an end. It would seem that the relativity of historical thought to the social environment was absolute; and
in that case it would be useless to gaze any longer at the
moving film of historical literature in the hope of discerning
in it the lineaments of some abiding form. . . . That conclusion, however, does not yet confront us. So far, we have
simply found that in the foreground of historical thought
there is a shimmer of relativity, and it is not impossible that
the ascertainment of this fact may prove to be the first step
towards ascertaining the presence of some constant and absolute object of historical thought in the background.[1]

The distinction hinted here leads right into the problem
of Orders of Ministers as determinable from history. Let us
see how this is so. We take nothing from what was said pre-
viously of Christianity's historical actuality. Jesus came into
history, the realm of man, and in Him God tabernacled in
history. Christianity can never escape this moment of its
origin. Nevertheless it is possible to overplay Christianity's
historical character and to make a false balance of histori-
city and the non-historical in the formation and being of it.

The *substance* of Christianity is not historical in the way
sometimes asserted. Christianity owes its substance as ultimately its origin to That which was before history and came
into it, to history as made by the Coming. Here we bring
to bear Toynbee's distinction between the "relative" and
the "constant or absolute" in historical inquiry. The
divine Word that came into history would itself be the

[1] *A Study of History*, I, pp. 15, 16.

"constant and absolute" factor in the history it entered and determined. The other factors were there, the things that make relative or circumstantial history as well as those belonging to the constant or essential. But if these two, the constant or essential and the circumstantial, are different-iable generally in history, how much more will this be so with God at the heart of history to re-form its essence and rehabilitate its order?

So that when Professor Fairweather says: "It makes a real difference to Christianity in every age that God came to the world when and where He did . . . the Christianized elements of Jewish custom from which the Catholic order developed have an enduring significance,"[1] we wholly agree; but would ask regarding the *sphere within history* of this significance and difference. The divine Coming itself altered history's inner content; but it would require a philosophy of history deriving history mainly from social causes, a "sociology of history" if we may borrow from the analogy of "sociology of knowledge," to make "Jewish custom" or any other social elements similarly determin-ing. On any other view, certainly as seen from Toynbee's distinction, this social area falls into place as the field where the "constant and absolute" factor is worked out; it is not directly of that factor. Comprising the time and attendant circumstances of the Incarnation rather than its proper nature, this area is the scene of secondary agencies the differences caused by which are also secondary, compared to those that arise immediately from the Divine Enactment. It is thus that in identifying the historical sphere of the differ-ences we discern their quality. They are real differences but they are not of the irreplaceable essence of Incarnation history.

If this is so, then Orders of Ministers or any Church Institutes emergent as to their form from "Jewish custom" or other social or even ecclesiastical background orderings cannot share the primacy that belongs to Christ Himself. Believers in Apostolic Succession would not claim that they do, though their language sometimes approaches this; for

[1] *supra*, p. 16.

example, the words of Pittenger in one of our earlier sections: "The supreme and crucial act of God for men is not Christ alone . . . it is Christ-Church."[1] What upholders of Apostolic Succession at the minimum do hold is that Christ instituted a Ministry and that this same Ministry ought to be permanent. No one would desire to discontinue an effective Ministry; but the question now is doctrinal. If our distinction of the essential and the circumstantial in respect of history has any force, then a relativity, in principle a transiency, befits the circumstantial that is forbidden to the other; and given this, and keeping in mind the way Apostolic Succession roots the form of the Ministry in Jewish practice and other strata of the circumstantial, it is hard not to feel that this doctrine of Succession, in making certain orders of Ministry ' essential,' comes near to reproducing in its own area the error of the literalist or fundamentalist who asks, for vehicles that have long and effectually served the Reality, the homage due to the Reality. Some of the vehicles may be appropriate to the service to the end of time, so not transitory in that dimension; but qualitatively they have a contingency which the Reality they bear has not. The earthen vessels remain earthen though they contain the heavenly Treasure.

We saw above how this about earthen vessels can become a plea for Apostolicity in bishops who were unspiritual (not the only ministers so to be); it has been a cover for much besides this unspirituality. What it *un*covers is this: unspiritual or spiritual, faithful or unfaithful, the vessels are and continue vessels; they are not as bearing the Treasure transubstantiated to the essence of it. Treasure and vessel are of the same species as our other distinction of essential and circumstantial history. In linking Orders of Ministers to the background of Jewish order, the doctrine of Apostolic Succession sets them by its own showing on the vessel-circumstantially-conditioned side of this double distinction, and only at the cost of self-consistency can it make what is peculiarly of the other or Treasure-Essence side a necessary attribute or enduement of these Orders.

[1] *supra*, p. 19.

Our purpose in distinguishing essential and circumstantial history is not to relegate the latter to unimportance. History is woven from circumstances; it is the composite of the trial and error and accomplishment of many generations. As bare essence it is non-existent and unthinkable. The circumstantial can reach high validity; in Christian history much that has emerged and become established, even if not of the 'essence' or indispensable to Christianity's being, is nonetheless of vast and living consequence. It is from this that one of the treasuries of faith is the reverence for Tradition and the realization of its place in the Church's life. Episcopacy is certainly among the things meriting this reverence and whose actual part in the Church gives them durable hold. Few would envisage the future of Christianity without Episcopacy, whatever changes in Church form may occur.

Yet giving this its full weight it still remains true that, besides what may be highly momentous in Christian history, there are the essentials or absolutes without which this history, Christianity itself, would not have been. Christ Himself is the sum of these; nothing else has the absolute quality or pure necessity that pertains to Him. He is the Fount of all, of the Church, the Ministry, the Fellowship. Episcopacy we can be certain expresses the Fellowship, but it does not determine it; it is His Spirit that determines. Whence an aptness in Streeter's words: "It may be that the line of advance for the Church of today is not to imitate the forms but to recapture the spirit of the Primitive Church—a spirit favourable to experiment."[1]

Perhaps 'forms' matter more than Streeter's context suggests; we have assented to the position that the Jewish environment of early Christianity in helping to shape its forms contributed permanently to its order. But this is not to accord to this contribution comparable import with what Christianity comprised as within itself. That the time and place when and where the Incarnation occurred affected the order of Christianity for every age, is true; but by the same token if Christianity had arisen at another time and place,

[1] *The Primitive Church*, p. 262.

its order would have been differently—though again permanently—influenced. Yet it would still be Christianity,
in any or every time and place, given the same Christ. Thus
it would appear that in what Christianity took from
"Jewish custom"—as in what it would have received from
any other *milieu*—there is something we can suitably term
accidental; and, enter into the making of Christianity as it
may, it is of its nature as mediated in history but not of
its integral nature. This is our distinction again of the
essential and the circumstantial; and it reveals orders of
Ministry, of the circumstantial in reflecting the Jewish
environment within which they emerged, as historically
valid (the circumstantial we maintained is real history). But
also historically relative by the primacy of the essential.
Neither Episcopacy, then, nor any other order of Ministry
is of the *esse* of Christianity as the essential has been conceived in these paragraphs. Christ is the essential, and
Episcopacy with other Ministries has essentiality to the
measure of its fidelity to Him.

This leads on to a second note in our critique of Apostolic
Episcopal Succession, one that is kindred to the first and
will reinforce the considerations offered in connection with
it.

In proceeding to our first criticism we distinguished
internal or essential and external or circumstantial history.
We shall now call to our aid an analogous distinction
between primary and, if the phrase can be forgiven, contingent necessity. This will be in relation to the position
of those who regard Episcopacy wearing the mantle of the
Apostles as necessary to the Church, the Church's essential
Ministry.

We have had before us in previous chapters the argument of those who uphold Apostolic Succession on account
of its service or even necessity to certain ends and objectives
of decisive import in the Church's work and life. It cost us
no strain to take these ends into appreciative regard. But it
is clear once the matter occurs, that what is prized as tribu-
tary or even necessary to ends must be secondary to the

ends. It cannot itself have the claim of first necessity.

Hence then our differentiation of primary and contingent or instrumental necessity. In reference to our subject we apply it thus. Episcopacy is regarded by believers in Apostolic Episcopal Succession as the guardian of the Truth, the Christian Word. Charged with so high a function Episcopacy is appropriately viewed as necessary. But the end-term of its necessity will be not in itself but in the Word. It will be necessary instrumentally or as means, however—believing it to be the true means—one may assert simply its necessity.

Defenders of Apostolic Episcopal Succession are not averse to this. To them Episcopacy *is* for function, as it was for the Church's vital functions it first came into being. It is not a sacrosanct institute in which function must be lodged whether it is the best agent for discharging it or not. But there is the possibility and often the subtle danger, when a thing is experienced as necessary to something else itself deemed wholly necessary, of forgetting this connection or contingence of the first thing's necessity and retaining in mind and even more in feeling just its necessity. What is 'necessary to' then becomes 'necessary' without qualifying reference. This danger has produced havoc in Christian thinking and hardly less in Christian spirituality. The spiritual order has its laws delicately interknit; one of them is that spiritual injury comes not always from what is bad or unspiritual, but from good things when they are felt to be so good, their service to the reality of so rare a quality, that they are made the reality. This snare waits stealthily for us in what is one of the most excellent of current religious happenings, the new common zeal for worship. Worship is the worship of God; but our fair worship appointments can themselves be so pleasing and seem so 'inspiring' that, as Forsyth warns, we come to think more of worship than we think of God.

If it is asked, Is something of this sort possible in the instance of Episcopacy in its relation to the end it subserves? we can, I think, have guidance toward an answer in turning again to Irenaeus.

In our former reference we gave passages from him that seem a *locus classicus* of Apostolic Succession as it has come down in the Catholic tradition. With no commonly received authoritative standard in New Testament Scripture, Irenaeus, when the stake is the Gospel, the thing which matters most, looks to the Apostolic Sees. It is historically a strong pillar of Catholic authority and order that before the norm was defined which to the Reformers was sole and sufficient, the *regula fidei* was the tradition of the Apostles preserved through the Church and the Catholic Ministry.

But for Irenaeus at least this tradition was not to be received blindly. He prescribes this test for what purports to be of it:

> Those who are believed to be presbyters, but . . . do not place the fear of God supreme in their hearts, but conduct themselves with contempt toward others, and are puffed up with the pride of holding the chief seat . . . shall be convicted by the Word . . . From all such persons it behoves us to keep aloof, but to adhere to those who hold the doctrine of the Apostles. . . . Where the gifts of the Lord have been placed, there it behoves us to learn the truth, from those who possess that succession which is from the Apostles, and among whom exists that which is sound and blameless in conduct, as well as that which is unadulterated and incorrupt in speech.[1]

Here the truth still comes through descent from the Apostles, but light is cast on the character of the descent. Those " believed to be presbyters " of whom Irenaeus is doubtful are to be " convicted by the Word." The Word is " the doctrine of the Apostles " and those who hold it are in " the succession from the Apostles." This makes descent from the Apostles to lie centrally, not in successive conferments of orders, but in the passing from one to another of the Apostles' Word. Succession is not extrinsic to the Word; it is not that certain ones having in the formal process of the Church succeeded to the Apostles will have the Word; but the other way, having the Word is to have succeeded.

[1] *op. cit.*, IV. 3, 4, 26.

Where the Word is, there are those who "possess the succession" and from whom we "learn the truth."

That to stand in the Apostles' order is not enough of itself becomes certain when we see it required of those so standing that they be "sound and blameless in life and unadulterated and incorrupt in speech." This is the test we are mentioning: Ministry down the ordered channel is authoritative for Irenaeus if it has and lives by the Word. The Word is his real concern. The Church being in the throes of disintegration, the New Testament Canon and the Great Councils that would give credal embodiment to the Rule of Faith being not yet, he turned to men in formal lineage from the Apostles; who so likely to hold their doctrine? But the doctrine was the end, looking to these men was method or means. Irenaeus leans chiefly on Episcopacy in this lineage; yet just to the measure of its being for the doctrine is his care for it. It is not in his immediate intention to set Episcopacy as an Order of Ministry above other Orders; but to separate all Ministers who uphold the Apostolic Faith from those who are in effectual schism through "making their own assemblies" in which to teach the pseudo-Gospel that is rending the Church. It is these schismatics or false teachers who are to be "convicted by the Word," the Word learned from those in whom "the gifts of the Lord have been placed"; from bishops because or in so far as they are first among the possessors of these gifts.

If this was the mind of Irenaeus as he sought to steer the Church of his day through her "sea of troubles", it counsels caution before making him or any of these early patristic writers patrons of the idea that Episcopacy is *jus divinum* in or as itself. Episcopacy—in the seat of the Apostles—holds the seal by its fealty to their Word and under the high probability or presumptive certainty that the faithful transmission of the Word can be entrusted to it. But should it fail, betray the Word or deviate from it, then the Word is its judge, it is 'convicted' by it; Episcopacy is under this judgment equally with other Ministries. Irenaeus has a sure instinct for the values of purity and integrity of the Faith

H

and of the Body that have generally shaped and buttressed the argument for Apostolic Ministry. The values are essential and irreplaceable; the necessity of the Ministry ensues from its service to them. Here, then, is the help that Irenaeus offers us in considering the relation of Episcopacy to its end or function, or in applying to the problem of Episcopacy our distinction of types of necessity. Apostolic Episcopacy is necessary not of itself but for the Church's Faith and Life; to these belong absolute and pure necessity. The successors of the Apostles are to be heeded not *as* successors but as this relation makes them the repositories of the Apostles' teaching. This points an extremely vital difference, that is negated when Orders of Ministers and the Truth itself are made coordinate ("twin pillars") instead of the first being instrument of the other, when Episcopacy or any formal Ministry is endued with end-necessity as itself essential to the Church's true being.

The essential is the Gospel as the Gospel of God. Episcopacy has served the Gospel to the measure that gives it, as before averred, full title to Christian reverence. But it falls under the rubric of all Ministries: it is the "servant of the Word" and it is the "essential Ministry" only if the Word cannot be served without it as sufficiently for the Word's essential ends as it can be with it. This could be the case, but who can demonstrate it and do full justice to the records of other Ministries? All Ministries of the Word are fruitful; all too are saddled with human liability and frailty. This is one "parity of ministers" none can gainsay: every minister is man and not God. "The Word is God" (John 1: 1), but not so the servant of the Word whatever his degree or consecration. All degrees are levelled under the sovereignty of the Word; whence the following:

> What we who are Protestants must say in the light of our own history and traditions, the continued blessing of God on Protestant missionary labours, and the signs of growth in Christian character and sanctity which have been given to us throughout our history as separated bodies, is what Christians must always confess in humility of the whole Church of Christ . . . This work is not of ourselves; it is the gift of God.

... We ask those in the older communions ... to consider the patent spiritual facts. If God has poured out His Spirit on our communions [recall Irenaeus' "where the gifts of the Lord have been placed"], if in all of them the fruit of the presence of the Holy Spirit is manifestly given ... if our alleged 'irregularities' or 'invalidities' have not barred us from the grace of our Lord who meets us in our Eucharists, and crowns our proclamation of the Word by drawing men and women all over the world out of darkness into light, who is there, of all those who bow in reverence before Him, that can deny to us the mark of Catholicity?[1]

This is pointedly said. For that the Church's essential or even regular Ministry is that of bishops and others ordained by them, is not established from Christian history through any straight coincidence of this Ministry and spiritual efficacy or evidence that the work is of God. It would require, for example, utter ignorance of the period to contend that in the sixteenth century the episcopal heirs of the Apostles one and all excelled in spiritual dynamic certain others who by this formal criterion were non-Apostolic. God did not in that epochal time repair to the one ministerial order for agents through whom to translate His mind into the actual shaping of history. In the evangelical awakening of the eighteenth century, the episcopally ordained, the Wesleys and others, were joined by many not in episcopal orders; while some on whom bishops' hands had been laid, including certain bishops themselves, sought to quell the stir. Then Spurgeon's great ministry, those of Dale of Birmingham, D. L. Moody and J. H. Jowett: were they deficient compared to those of their episcopally ordained confrères? Were they not, if human ministries can be, valid ministries? The ministries of Henry Ward Beecher in Brooklyn and Phillips Brooks in Boston are universally acknowledged to have been spiritually productive; if a strict comparison revealed a margin of spiritual productivity, would any portion of it be attributable to the fact that the one was episcopally ordained, the other not?

[1] Flew and Davies in *The Catholicity of Protestantism*, p. 20.

But we must watch lest this argument prove too much. Its premiss appears to be that what makes a minister is divine enduement for his work, and signs are lacking that episcopally ordained ministers as a body have had this enduement in significant ways denied to other ministers. But making the tests those of Dr. Flew, we can go farther. There have been laymen under whose preaching the things happened that he enumerates: men were "drawn from darkness to light" and the change was permanent. These preachers were mighty in word and prayer; divine power was unquestionably with them.

Hence a polemic resting on "where the gifts of the Lord have been placed" could go beyond episcopal ordination *versus* other ordination to question the necessity of any ordination; save for orderliness or practical convenience in carrying on the Church's work.

This ushers us into a way of thinking about the Ministry that many find attractive and that easily enlists New Testament support. Are not all believers ministers or even priests (Rev. 1: 6), called to minister one to another according to the grace ($\chi \acute{\alpha} \rho \iota s$) given to them (Rom. 12: 5, 6)? Clearly there is in the New Testament this ministry of 'gifts' or charismatic ministry, "not as a secondary formal ministry comparable to the institutional ministry,"[1] but the ministry of all. "There are diversities of gifts . . . but to *every man* is given the manifestation of the Spirit to profit withal" (I Cor. 12: 4, 7). Or as in another place: *Every one* that heareth is to say, Come, to sound the Gospel call, in chorus with the Spirit and the Bride (Rev. 22: 17).

Given, however, all this, it in no way impairs the other fact that has come to view in our inquiry: as definitely as the $\chi \alpha \rho \acute{\iota} \sigma \mu \alpha \tau \alpha$ all are exhorted to covet (I Cor. 12: 31), the New Testament knows the special Gift of Ministry: of the Apostles and of Paul as an Apostle, not in the general sense in which all Christians are 'sent,' but 'separated' unto Apostleship; of the elders ordained by the Apostles (Acts 14: 23; Titus 1: 5): of deacons, perhaps of others,

[1] Ehrhardt, *The Apostolic Succession in the First Two Centuries of the Church*, p. 100.

also set apart (Phil. 1: 1; I Tim. 3: 8 ff.; 5: 1 ff.). The ministry of all in the New Testament Church is of its life; Paul in the passages Rom. 12: 4 ff. and I Cor. 12: 1 ff. is the expositor of it; but not as himself a case of it. He can admonish other ministers and lay on all in the Church the common ministry, as being himself Minister not at man's call or admonishing, but through the will of God (I Cor. 1: 1).

As well, then, as "the priesthood of *all* believers" there is, if we follow the New Testament, a Ministry in which God "sets *some*" (I Cor. 12: 28; Eph. 4: 11). To reason, therefore, to the non-necessity of an ordained Ministry from the fact that God's Word reaches men through preachers who are not ordained, is not required by the New Testament; nor that nothing pertains to this Ministry not possessed by the believing body. The common ministry is vital; the Church today is the poorer in having lost it as it obtained when the Church was articulate in prayer and witness through its members as well as its Ministers. Yet equally certain is this other: there was from the first the specially chosen Ministry expressly charged, not only with preaching the Word (Mk. 3: 13, 14; Mt. 10: 7; Lk. 9: 2; Acts 6: 4), but with guarding it from perversion and with building up and establishing the Church in it (Acts 2: 42; Eph. 4: 11-13; I Tim. 6: 20). This Ministry appears in the Apostles and extends to those who with and following the Apostles receive this same charge (I Cor. 15: 3; 2 Tim. 2: 2).

It is this Ministry we are considering in this work, and we are thinking just now of its process down the Church's history. Many would say that this Ministry itself, as it began in the Apostles and has continued in all who coming after them have preached the Word, is the real Apostolic Succession. But we are examining Apostolic Episcopal Succession, the belief that this procession of Apostolic Ministry has been channelled to the one institutional and historical course. It is necessary to focus the issue in this specific form. Ministers of non-episcopal Churches have been heard to say almost jauntily, "I am in the Apostolic Succession! "

117

They mean that in their time and place they preach the Word as did the Apostles. By their view of the Ministry their boast may be true; but it doesn't meet the contention over Apostolic Succession which centres in the belief, not that there are always preachers in the Church whose Gospel is that of the Apostles, but that Apostleship itself belongs to certain ones or to a certain order among them through their being Successors of the Apostles when the latter, as in the New Testament, are also seen as not coterminous with the body of the Church's servants and helpers but as a special Ministry within or over it. This certain order is that of the bishops, with, linked to them in the Succession, the other Ministries to which they ordain.

This is the belief against which in this chapter we are bringing the criticism that it inadmissibly crosses the line of distinctions it is essential, as we see it, to observe: those between integral and circumstantial history and between first and secondary necessity. Under the second of these distinctions, we are judging Episcopacy to be necessary just insofar as it is so for the ends of the Word or for the Church's vocation in the world; no more than other Ministries is it of intrinsic necessity. In regard to history, we employed Toynbee's differentiation of environmentally moulded history and history as enshrining an absolute object for thought. We found no cause to deny that the time-incidence of the Incarnation did affect the historical selection of materials in the making of Christianity as a movement in history; these materials, largely from Jewish precedents, became permanent constituents of historical Christianity. But it consorts with Toynbee's differentiation (in our terms, with the distinction between essential and circumstantial history) to refuse to what is fashioned from historical and social relativities a place in the being of Christianity or a role in its working comparable to that which belongs to what has come into history straight from the Incarnation and points back as necessarily to its transcendent Cause. Forms of Ministry, Episcopal and other, however high the background agencies whence they emerged, however they have become practically indispensable through the way history has gone, still are not of the absolute in history's structure. For to Christian theology history is *Heilsgeschichte,* the History of Salvation in Tillich's phrase, or in Cullmann's, Redemptive History; and since we are not redeemed by forms and orders they cannot be of the *esse* of that history—that status is for the divine redemptive activity itself—though history's own causality may have made them a perpetual part of it.

Our criticisms of Apostolic Episcopacy invite the answer of those for whom the issue does not hang on the emanation of Episcopacy from God's work in the Incarnation, whereby it is of the substance of Christianity's historical being. Let it suffice, we hear them say, that the Episcopal Ministry was divinely willed of itself and it exists in the Church by express design as God's appointed medium of His grace to men.

This support of Apostolic Episcopal Succession incurs in its turn the charge of pushing the problem down to the character of God. Is it consistent with Christianity's conception of God to predicate of Him exclusive reliance on some one ministerial order? Would not the result, that men possess His grace, be the interest for Him, to the degree whence He would employ freely the agencies best adapted to it? "Those of us," writes Bishop Stephen Neill, "who reject the doctrine of the Church and Ministry set forth in *The Apostolic Ministry,* reject it, not on grounds of minute differences on points of archaeological interpretation, but because we cannot recognize as Christian the doctrine of God which seems to underlie this imposing theological edifice."[1] We mentioned on an earlier page the danger in this approach of making ourselves judge of what God would or would not do. The question as we then phrased it is, not what would God as we conceive Him be likely to do, but what has He done? We have instances of God's action to rule our thought of it, as well as our prior deductions. God did choose Israel, Christ did ordain the Apostles. If He

[1] *The Ministry of the Church,* p. 28.

decreed a Ministry for His Church, it is one more Deed or Dispensation not to be brought to account to our preconceptions which would have precluded former Deeds of God that are now part of the faith of the whole Christian world. We cannot, however, deny wholly the force of Bishop Neill's words and retain our distinction of pure and indirect necessity. God's purpose is the fulfilment of man's spirit, and a doctrine of God is other than Christian which represents Him as caring for ecclesiastical orders with the care He has for this fulfilment.

We are confident, then, of this: that God called a Ministry and gave authority to it, our confidence secure on the ground that God's doing thus coheres with other acts and stages of His historical working. But further than this we pause. When upholders of Apostolic Succession declare Episcopacy to be this Ministry divinely placed in history, they seem to us to step outside God's essential activity into the region of historical data and happenings which it is the role of historical research to appraise. And the appraisal is difficult for the reason, among others, that many of these data pertain to a period where our knowledge is sparse and what we have is indeterminate.

We have seen how naturally the Church, prior to possessing the New Testament canon, looked to the bishops. But the plea for the primacy of Episcopacy based upon this could be double-edged. For the conjecture becomes possible that the Church lacking full New Testament guidance missed her way. Harnack's story of the secularization of Christianity in the sub- and post-Apostolic eras is a hard morsel for those who lean for doctrine on these eras; the whole Catholic system could be symbol and sequel of this secularization. This is an issue we do not have to determine; but the uncertainties pertaining to the period in which Catholic Episcopacy emerged, the different constructions and valuations of developments in the Church within that period, persuade us of the impossibility of establishing as a *sure* historical decision that Apostolic Episcopacy is one of the structures of historical Christianity of specific divine authorization. The belief that it was so authorized and commanded is entangled with historical dilemmas we have not the means to resolve.

Here is a short summary of our examination and criticism of the doctrine of Apostolic Episcopal Succession:

Episcopacy as it arose in the Church unfolded naturally and legitimately from Christianity's historical beginnings. It came by understandable and valid steps to take the place at first held by the Apostles. But it does not share the primal Christian history as one of the ingredients without which it would not be *that* history, in the way this is so of Christ Himself, His work and victory, and the fellowship born of these. It was proper to Christianity's actual historical origin; but in another historical setting Christianity could have matured, become a full Christianity, without begetting Episcopacy. In the formation of the Ministry in the New Testament and the patristic Church, the central developments and their outcome show formally a close parallel to the demands of the Apostolic-Episcopal theory. Episcopacy did actually evolve to become the Church's authoritative and ascendant Ministry. The claims as to Episcopacy have all the validity that comes from this truth of history.

In a similar way our study has revealed the beginnings very early of the tendency to centre in the Apostles, and the bishops coming after them, the power to ordain;[1] this was the essential trend notwithstanding instances of ordination by those not known as Apostles. Nevertheless, neither Episcopacy nor Episcopal Ordination is ever in the earliest period ranked with things indispensable. These contrary instances bar this of themselves in respect of Ordination; and they are in company with the fact that, however Episcopacy and Episcopal Ordination would certainly come to be from the demands of the Church's work and the turn events received, not once within the New Testament or the Apostolic Church is it felt or laid down in regard to either of them that it must be. Our survey of the early history does everything for Episcopacy short of unveiling any sure marks

[1] *supra*, pp. 81, 82.

of its juridic necessity or of its being divinely enjoined.

The same observation holds of other Ministries. We saw in the Acts of the Apostles the Eldership moving definitely to become a permanent Ministry. Yet in the two places, I Cor. 12: 28 and Eph. 4: 11, where Paul lists the Ministers God "hath set" in the Church, Elders are not included; though any "argument from silence" resting on this is balanced by the fact that if the Epistle to the Ephesians does not mention Elders, we know from Acts 20: 17 ff. that there were Elders in the Ephesian Church endowed with the full pastoral commission (v. 28). All in all, the mood of the New Testament and of early Christianity, highly sensitive to the need for Ministry, seems little inclined towards legislating for that Ministry special titles and forms compared to its anxiety that it devote itself steadfastly to the work it has been created to fulfil.

This summary is not altered when we come farther down the annals of the Church. Episcopacy in the course of Christianity has played a foremost part; it has good claim to the title of the most illustrious of Ministries. Yet its functions as they are generally regarded have sometimes fallen to other Ministries, and have not been lost; the absolute necessity of Episcopacy is precluded again by the recorded effectiveness and fruitfulness of these other Ministries. Even where Episcopacy is believed to have been singularly instrumental, the field of unity and continuity, the facts are not of one order. Episcopacy did not prevent the Great Schism of East and West, nor the vast nonconforming secessions from Episcopal Churches in lands enjoying religious freedom. Yet Episcopacy has served the Church greatly and uniquely, and we can conceive no other Order constituting so readily a link of Ministry for a reunited Christendom; though this again is by its historical and present ecclesiastical prominence and influence, rather than of essential principle or of its quality *in se*.

Episcopacy is not of the core of Christianity as is the Gospel; there is no Christianity without the Gospel, but that Christianity can exist—has existed—with and without Episcopacy is open fact. Christianity, or the Church, may be more complete with Episcopacy; Episcopacy may be of its *plene esse* as its *bene esse*. But this further characterizes Christianity's world position as historically formed. Christianity's being of itself—its *esse*—does not connote Episcopacy. Episcopacy neither takes from that *esse* nor adds to it. God gave a Ministry for the Gospel but not tied to a special Order; Orders are not identical with Ministry *per se* but are its needed accessory for fulfilling it under modes which amid changing circumstances ensure this fulfilment. If Faith and Order are Christianity's "twin pillars" they are not equal twins. Faith could hardly give effect to itself in our world without Order; but Order is the servant, and however the servant be as its lord, it is not lord. Faith to Christianity is *sine qua non*; Order is given to Faith for its diffusion and action, and authoritative forms of Order (Orders of Ministry) are any whose virtue it is to have actualized the gift.

In outlining and examining the doctrine of Apostolic Episcopal Succession we have disclosed something of our own understanding of the Ministry's nature and purpose. Our remaining chapter will attempt their more explicit delineation with a view to reaching, in the process, a statement of the Doctrine of the Ministry to which our inquiry will have led.

Chapter 4

THE DOCTRINE OF THE MINISTRY: A STATEMENT FOR THE CHURCH TODAY

OUR consideration of the Biblical data pertaining to the Ministry, and of the development of the Ministry in the early Christian centuries; the principles of the Ministry we have derived from these studies, all mean nothing if they have not persuaded us of this: the sources of the Ministry lie deep in the counsels of God and in the movement of God in history. Jesus at the midpoint of that movement calls the Ministry into being for the service of it; He does this as the One come from God to fulfil the movement. Thus the Ministry is first not of man but of God and of the will of Christ. We have put it into the positive scale in weighing Apostolic Episcopal Succession that it acknowledges this transcendent import of the Ministry and has steadfastly held the Church and the Ministry to it. It is no doctrine of the Ministry that does not include this divine stratum of its formation and being and make it determining. Bereft of it, the Ministry is an anomaly: as a bare human career or employment the most pedestrian and purposeless of all.

This is our outlook upon the Ministry in general form at this turn of our inquiry. We go on to attempt in detailed order a statement of the Doctrine of the Ministry as it comes from filling in and explicating this basal position.

I

The Ministry Distinct in Being and Function

There is a tendency in some who write on the subject of

the Ministry to keep the Ministry to its definition by emphasizing the role of the Church. Examples are these:

When the Apostles who had been sent out by Jesus had discharged their task, they returned to Jesus who had bestowed it upon them. After the Resurrection an entirely new situation had arisen, and a new commission was necessary. The new ' Apostolate' was confined to those who had been eye-witnesses of the Resurrection, including the Eleven, but also many others. The function of these ' Apostles' was to witness to the Resurrection; and, from the nature of the case, it was unique and unrepeatable. These ' Apostles' were the Apostles of Christ in His Church, and when they died or were killed their unique functions reverted to Him. Thus it is the whole Church of Christ, in which He dwells, and not a particular body of men, which succeeds to the Apostolic Ministry, and the whole Church has that Ministry today.[1]

To what do the successors of the Apostles succeed? . . . not to the special status involved in our Lord's promise to the Twelve. Equally it is not to the quality of having been an eye-witness of the foundation facts of the faith from John's Baptism to the Resurrection. That quality ceased with the first generation of Christians: it also was not transmissible. What is left? So far as I can see, three things: the need of the world, the call of Christ, and the tradition of His Ministry in the flesh in Galilee and Judaea and in the Church which is His Body throughout the world. And, so far as I can see, it is the Church that succeeds to these things. The Church is apostolic because she is called by Christ and empowered and instructed by Christ to go and make disciples of the nations.[2]

These excerpts are vividly suggestive, but I cannot feel that they give the whole truth. They are right in what they affirm: Christ did call the Church and bequeath to it the things these passages severally name; the Church is Apostolic for the reasons they state. But this does not preclude a Ministry also sent of Christ, the inheritor of His gifts to

[1] Flew and Davies, *The Catholicity of Protestantism*, p. 105.
[2] Manson, *The Church's Ministry*, p. 52.

it. Christ raised up the Church, but we are told just as clearly He set *some* within it, for the edifying of the Church, for the work of the Ministry (I Cor. 12: 28; Eph. 4: 11, 12). Are all Apostles? asks Paul; are all teachers? The picture this from Paul seems to offer is not of the Church *rather than* the Ministry succeeding to what Christ bestowed; but of Church *and* Ministry sharing the bestowal, with the Ministry, though given to the Church, receiving its own commission as definitely as the Church.

This representation from Paul is corroborated by the facts of Christian beginnings. We have seen that Jesus very early created a Ministry when He ordained the Apostles and sent them out to preach and heal (Mk. 3: 14, 15; Mt. 10: 5-8). This Ministry continued after the Resurrection in the same Apostles who "ceased not to preach and teach" (Acts 5: 42), and in their fellow-labourers who "went everywhere preaching the Word" (8: 4). It is hard to follow the first of the above citations in its mention of a new commission after the Resurrection and a new Apostolate. The original commission was to preach the Word, the Kingdom of God (Lk. 9: 2). The Apostles who received this commission were to become under the dictum of events eyewitnesses of the Resurrection. No new Apostolate was summoned to witness to the Resurrection and then pass away. That witness fell to the first Apostles and to others who were eye-witnesses with them. The Resurrection stupendously altered their outlook and the theme of their teaching; but their commission was still to preach and it drew the Resurrection to it; whence "they preached Jesus and the Resurrection" (Acts 4: 2; 17: 18), as Ministers ever since have done.

The testifying by eye-witnesses to the Resurrection would be unique and temporary; with the last of the eye-witnesses it would, in the above writer's word, 'revert'. But the *preaching* of the Resurrection—the preaching of the Word —did not revert. Thus before and after the Resurrection it was the one Apostolate and commission, the Ministry of the Word. The Apostles fulfil this Ministry in the mission on which they are first sent out by Jesus (Mt. 10: 7; Lk. 9: 2,

6); they again fulfil it in the post-Resurrection Church (Acts 6: 2, 4), only now with vaster substance and consequence from the mighty accessions to the Word the first Easter Morn has brought.

Our tendency so far in this section has been to portray the Ministry as having place equally with the Church in Christ's primal provision; or even to suggest the Ministry's precedence of the Church as an historical episode. Precedence has no part when we are thinking of the Church as ideally transcendent and primordial, as in the instances given in our first chapter; it may mean little if in contemplating the Church's course in history the stress falls on its community of principle with the Old Testament People of God and the Israelitish Remnant. But in its historical manifestation as the Christian ἐκκλησία, the Church had its temporal moment making precedence assignable; there were other things prior to it. The Ministry arguably was one among them. Apart from the order implied in the much controverted Mt. 16: 18—the confessing Apostle (Minister), *then* the Church built upon him or upon his confession—there is the assured datum of the Twelve, the firstborn of Christian Ministries, well forward in the Record of any naming of the Church. The Church may be thought to have begun when others gathered about the Twelve and about Jesus Himself; the company of these would make a loose semblance of what was afterwards the Church. It is common to place the proper era of the Church in the period of the Resurrection. "The Church," says Lietzmann, "arose in Jerusalem; Christ appeared to the five hundred brethren in connection with Pentecost, and this led to the founding of the Church."[1] It is this Church, born of the Resurrection and of the Gift of the Spirit, that has had historical and corporate continuance down to our own day.

Our point of present interest is that, on any of these views of the first emergence of the Church, the Ministry was there before it. Even after the Resurrection it was to Ministers (the Eleven Apostles) that Jesus left His trust: the com-

---

[1] *The Beginnings of the Christian Church*, V.

mand to "teach all nations" which Dr. Manson mentions as addressed to the Church was laid upon them (Mt. 28: 16-20), as were the solemn admonitions and assurances, all from the Risen Christ, of Mk. 16: 14-18; John 20: 19-23; 21: 15-17; Acts 1: 2-8. As Christians multiply in the days following Pentecost they are still a group gathered about the Ministry ("they continue in the Apostles' doctrine and fellowship", Acts 2: 42), however promptly they mature into a Church (v. 47).

This chronological precedence of the Ministry, however, is nothing of itself. It no longer stands if, taking the course that many favour, we trace the Church back beyond the other possible beginning-points at which we hinted to Jesus' choice of the disciples and make His calling of them, equally with being the epoch of the Ministry, the nascent stage of the Church. Our reason for referring to the priority of the Ministry is not any importance it can have *per se*, but the value for our present contention of the circumstances, as they have just been before us, that prompt the suggestion of it. For these circumstances, if they do not persuade us of the Ministry's prior being, do at least imply its being; they reveal the Ministry as of Christianity's pristine order; not a convenient addendum for practical effectiveness, but itself within the structure of what God did, integral to the whole redemptive economy wrought out through Israel and through Christianity as the spiritual Israel. The Ministry is of the substance Christ brought to the shadow; of the Second Thing, to establish which He took away the first (Heb. 10: 1, 9). It was itself willed and appointed by Christ as He willed and endued the Church.

Some will apprehend in this attributing of distinct entity, not to say historical primacy, to the Ministry, the embryo of Clericalism, the ecclesiastical order within which the ministerial hierarchy is the actuality of the Church, the people being the 'faithful' girt in obedience about it. This, however, would altogether misconceive our approach. The Ministry whenever and however arising is not for dominance but service. The Apostles at the first are sent as harbingers of the Kingdom which is not peculiarly theirs but is for all to whom they offer salvation within it. Then when the Church has come to formal being they are servants of it, or as its leaders they direct it to a fulfilment which again is not special to themselves but is one for all. Grant freely to the Ministry being of itself, even that it received this being when as yet the Church as the institutionalized Christian Church was not; yet it is not functionally *for* itself. It is, always and only, for the divine purpose which, however it employs special agencies, awards nothing to them save to have their portion in a Perfection to which the many too are called and which finally is for none without the others (Heb. 11: 40).

Thus the Ministry does not acquire 'rank' in having its own being and calling. Be not called Rabbi, commands Jesus; ye are all brethren (Mt. 23: 1-12). Nevertheless the Ministry is exalted, only to another scale. The manner of its exaltation is this. The Ministry we have said is distinct, or in Paul's word 'separated.' But the separation is positive in the Church's life, not divisive. It is separation not *from* (the wider communion), but *unto* the common Gospel (Rom. 1: 1, 16). Separation is the divine ordainment and quality of the Ministry for service to all who are called in the Gospel, not for being raised officiously above them. Yet the Ministry is 'raised' in being called to the service; not, however, to status but to the high station and 'greatness' Jesus knew to be intrinsic to service, to the calling of Minister (Mk. 10: 43, 44); raised too to position and place, not to be "lords of God's heritage" but to be "free from men" (I Cor. 9: 19) in ministering God's will to them obediently to His call.

This, then, is our first word: the Ministry has its own designation and God-given charge. However it be by consent and act of the Church, it is initially "the Lord's doing"; God is first in the making of a Minister. The Minister has nothing from prerogative or preferment but everything from this: he is where he is through the decision of God. So was Paul a Minister: not of men, neither by man, but by Jesus Christ and God the Father (Gal. 1: 1).

There would be in this beginning of our Doctrine,

though it had nothing more, all the Minister can ask for his imperative and commitment. To Paul it sufficed for all, this being Minister "through the will of God"; "woe, then, is me if I preach not the Gospel" (I Cor. 9: 16). A man at the start of life may choose from among the 'professions'; choosing the Ministry, he may later reconsider: circumstances may appear to justify turning to some other, perhaps more lucrative, avocation. We are not his judge; but what effectually pertains to decision and redecision thus his own act, if it is God who decides (or has decided), whence again as with Paul, "necessity is laid upon me" (*ibid.*)? The Minister—or any one—facing the issue of himself and his life-work is secure in his choice for himself if he have prior acquaintance with the divine choice for him. "Ye have not chosen me, but I have chosen you" (John 15: 16). Nothing so surely and basically belongs to the Ministry or the Doctrine of the Ministry as this election and constraint of God.

This first stage in outlining our Doctrine having thus confirmed to our mind the Minister divinely chosen and sent, it will be appropriate to it to give our final considered word on the worth and force of the *shaliach* conception for our thinking upon the Ministry. Upholders of Apostolic Succession sometimes apply this conception in ways not helpful to their cause. They rely on it for support of 'Succession' and are then easily discomfited when it is shown how unlikely under Jewish law would be the devolving of the *shaliach's* mandate. "The *shaliach* has a definite commission . . . his authority does not extend beyond his terms of reference and lapses when the commission has been executed."[1] Another writer's inference from this and other connected facts is that "the discarding of the *shaliach* hypothesis is of great importance for the doctrine of the Apostolic Succession."[2]

Our judgment would endorse the impertinency of the *shaliach* principle to the 'Succession' side of Apostolic Succession, but retain it for its other term, Apostolicity. For *shaliach*, the sent who is one with the sender, does

[1] Manson, *op. cit.*, p. 37.
[2] Ehrhardt, *op. cit.*, p. 19.

instance the type of unity of Christ and the Apostles; we saw how "he that receiveth you receiveth me" was His repeated address to them. The character of the Ministry as Apostolic is illumined from this *shaliach* relation, not through the mere verbal identity of 'apostle' and '*shaliach*', but in that the relation—generally as we have seen, vividly as comprised in these words of Christ to His first Ministers—bodies forth both the divine ground of the Ministry and the *personal* bond which links the Minister to Him by whom he is commissioned. *Shaliach* contracts to a term the Biblical presentation of the Minister as not alone in office but *personally* joined to the One by whom he is sent and empowered. It is thus the values of *shaliach* can be woven into our thought of the Ministry, not for anything they yield to the issue of Succession—on which we have yet to give our summary finding—but for the help they afford this first note of our Doctrine, the Ministry itself divinely conceived, and for the way they enforce the unity of the Ministry with Christ and enrich the meaning of that unity.

We shall speak later of the Minister as the chosen instrument of the Church and of the confirmation of His call by the Church. At the moment our thought is of the deeper fact: the Ministry's final *raison d'être* in God's will and purpose, for the sake of which it is given to the Church. We have been citing the *shaliach*-idea as illuminative of this. But how far it is so is not of chief account; what matters is the momentous truth itself: the Ministry from God to herald His Kingdom, from Christ, the emissary and delegate of His reconciling office (2 Cor. 5: 19, 20). It is no Christian Ministry where this is not felt, under the press of God's compulsion and in amazement at the mystery in which one who is a Minister after this calling stands involved, and which has validation and answer not in "scheme and plan" but only in humble certainty of what God hath planned, and more, what God hath wrought.

So the first tier of our Doctrine: the Ministry God's proper handiwork and appointed agency for making known and confirming in men the saving, all-sufficing Word He

THE DOCTRINE OF THE MINISTRY

has given them to hear. "How shall they hear without a preacher?" The Church is begotten of the Word the Ministry proclaims and adds her own testimony to it. But the proclamation is foundational; whether or not the Ministry itself is prior, nothing antecedes its function. God's first interest is not that an institution be spread over the world, but that the Gospel be preached to all nations (Mk. 13: 10; 16: 15; Mt. 28: 19). "How shall they preach except they be sent?" That there shall be those who are sent, God has given the Ministry, enduing it by His other Gift with the Word which mankind for its end in God must receive.

II

The Ministry and the Holy Spirit

The Holy Spirit is God Himself present and active in our human world. God was known in this mode of His presence and action before the advent of Christ; the Spirit came upon the prophets and was the "source of the old prophetic fire." The prophets, however, knew they did not have the Spirit in its fulness and pointed to the day when He would be given without measure (Joel 2: 28 ff.). Christians from the first have discerned this day in the period of the Resurrection when the infant Church received power for her mission and hailed the prophet's vision in the outpouring by which she knew her own Pentecost had fully come (Acts 1: 8; 2: 1-18).

Christians, however, again from the beginning, have seen this "gift of the Spirit" in fulness as the fulfilment, not of the prophet's word only, but of the expectation and promise of Jesus (Acts 2: 33; Lk. 24: 49; John 14: 16, 26). Secured by this promise, the experience of the Spirit has been realized as the presence of Jesus Himself in the Spirit, to abide to the end (John 14: 18 ff.; Mt. 28: 20). Thus the Holy Spirit is the assurance that God, who in Christ came to men in visible form, has not gone from them now He is no more seen. The Ascension was not God's withdrawal as

132

the Incarnation was His advent and visitation. He came to remain: if Jesus was Emmanuel, God with us, the Spirit is Paraclete, equally God with us or at our side (John 14: 17). The Holy Spirit is the ever-presence of the selfsame God who 'was' in Christ.

Jesus' pledge of the Paraclete reveals the link between the Ministry and the Holy Spirit. We saw before how He announces the same office for both: the Spirit will testify of Him, His Ministers having been with Him will also witness (John 15: 26, 27). But the Spirit does more than witness *with* the Ministry; it is His also to *enable* Ministers to witness, as in Acts 1: 8 where Ministers are equipped to witness in receiving the Spirit. Linking this enablement by the Spirit to the other fact that the Spirit Himself witnesses, the truth emerges that in empowering Ministers to witness the Spirit is endowing them with His own function, making them partners with Him in His essential work. This is the basis and principle of much else in the New Testament in which Holy Spirit and Ministry are placed in unison or actively conjoined. Thus the Spirit is 'given' (John 7: 39); God also 'gave' the Ministry (Eph. 4: 11). The Spirit guides the disciples into all truth and glorifies Christ (John 16: 13, 14); the Ministry is for edifying and perfecting of the saints in knowledge unto the fulness of Christ (Eph. 4: 12, 13). The Spirit brings all things to 'remembrance' (John 14: 26); Paul exhorts Timothy whom he has made a Minister to put the Church in 'remembrance' of the things of faith (2 Tim. 2: 14). Spirit and Ministry alike teach the Word (John 14: 26; I Cor. 2: 7-11; Mt. 28: 20; 2 Tim. 2: 2 and the numerous other New Testament references to the Ministry's teaching office). Taken in whole, these points bespeak substantial identity of function of the Ministry and the Holy Spirit.

Not that they are equal in the function; the function integrally is that of the Spirit. The Spirit chooses and consecrates a human medium for His own operation. The Ministry is born of this action of the Spirit and continually renewed to the Church by it. The Spirit's function becomes the Minister's directly in his being given the Spirit; the gift of the Spirit, that is, is not the Minister, his function already apportioned to him, receiving empowerment for it, but it is his being given the function with empowerment inherent to the gift. Thus the prophet was *anointed* to preach, not just enabled, in the Spirit's being upon him: enabled in being anointed (Isa. 61: 1; cf. Lk. 4: 18); thus they spake at Pentecost as the Spirit gave them utterance (Acts 2: 4), sealing thereby the pledge of Jesus given just before (1: 8) that authorization to witness and power for it would alike be theirs through the bestowal of the Spirit. Paul also knew his preaching itself as well as its power was of the Spirit: "my speech was in demonstration of the Spirit that your faith should stand not in the wisdom of men, but in the power of God" (I Cor. 2: 4, 5). Wisdom and power are here synonymous or co-ordinate requisites for the preacher obtained through equal action of the Spirit.

This affords for our Doctrine of the Ministry the truth very near its heart: the Ministry and the Holy Spirit are one in vocation and power through the Minister's single enduement with these as they pertain to the Spirit and are indissolubly one in Him. The Minister's task is that of the Spirit by common definition: the Spirit witnesses to 'me' (John 15: 26); ye shall be 'my' witnesses (Acts 1: 8). Not that this implies parallelism of the Ministry and the Spirit; our main emphasis in this section is that the Ministry has the task in first having the Spirit: "after the Spirit is come upon you, ye shall witness" (*ibid.*). Unity in witness of the Ministry and the Spirit is not agreement of concurrent witnessings, but the Spirit's indwelling making the Minister's witnessing identically that of the Spirit (Acts 5: 32: "we are witnesses of these things as is the Holy Spirit whom God has given"; cf. Rom. 8: 9-11). Thus for the Minister to live as Minister is the Holy Spirit, even as being ordained by the Spirit and made meet for the work in having His power is the essence of Ministry. The work being of God must be done in the power of God and directed by Him.

Such is Christian belief averred everywhere by the Churches. But the modern world is sceptical and dismisses all this about the Spirit, divine or supernatural power, as antique mythology which knowledge has outdistanced. Psychology has revealed there is always power in ego-transcending devotion; to be joined with others in self-forgetting abandon to an end mutually deemed worthy of this uncalculating commitment has its complement of power in inwardly unifying those so committed, to the release within them of unsuspected stores of energy and fervour. This can happen in relation to any cause capable of being sufficiently compelling; multitudes today have found in sectional revolutionary ardour an escape from inner discord and a spiritual translation from a low level of futility and aimlessness to an exalted one of zest for shared achievement, while themselves deriving rich reversion benefits of meaningfulness and victory in personal life.

There is no doubt of this, nor that psychology merits praise for what it has done to elucidate the springs and interconnections of personal power. There are Communists who evince far more 'power' than their Christian counterparts; one is accustomed to jeremiads over this from despondent Christians. But it is just here that Christians instead of being lugubrious should be re-searching their own first principles. Is power solely of this inwardly generated sort under the impact and demands of confronting situations? Was Pentecost, which brought the Church to self-awareness, the outcome of some inner integration through purely psychic adjustment which, occurring in members of an assembled company, quickened their feeling of being "all in one accord"? As to the Ministry: was the conversion of Paul, whence he became first of ministers and missionaries, the resolution in the Freudian style of a divided self, rampant within him from his continuing to persecute the Christians when the example of Stephen and various inner urges had shattered his confidence in that course? Is the "power of the Holy Spirit" whenever manifest resolvable in like fashion into psychic and other natural agents and states?

The Christian answer would be that for all of these the naturalistic and psychological account is insufficient. They

135

are not just instances of some common category of power, but have a residuum and a range that are *sui generis*. They are inexplicable in what is most characteristic and momentous in them, save through God's real action and the way men are reached by it. This Christian claim stands with other reasons that have been discerned for doubting this notion of homogeneous power. Men variously find divers orders of power, evil as well as good. Among the orders is God's power through the Holy Spirit, not reducible to the others nor commensurable with them.

Our world, however, no longer knows this; it has largely lost whatever persuasion it ever had of the reality of this supra-dimensional Power, this δύναμις unknown to human potency available in God. The rehabilitation of this persuasion will not come from theory; it can be hoped for only as there is had from the Church and the Ministry fresh practical proof of this Power and what is attainable through it. This in turn will require in the Church and among her people a resurgence of the distinctive Christian power-experience to which the Church's annals, especially her great epochs, bear speaking and convincing tribute; and a renewed conviction that the Church labours and prevails through divine power, never through devices and strategies that are perfectible apart from it. This simply and in a word is re-birth of faith in the Holy Spirit; and the fruit of it would be the re-born Church through her new-awakened certainty of the *actuality* of this Resource beyond all human power-contrivings, and her re-committal in dependence upon it—upon the Holy Spirit—not alone for success in her undertakings but for her existence and continuance. This divine power does not despise our human capabilities; it elicits and enlists "all that is within us" of purpose and response. But it superadds to this, and charges it with, its own great increment, the *gift* of the Holy Spirit. It is this that is the agent of divine Presence to the Church, not psychic-spiritual energies within ourselves. As in the Sacrament—the exemplar of this truth *par excellence* —when we confess Christ's Real spiritual Presence: this spiritual Presence is not Christ as we apprehend and feel

Him in our subjective spiritual states, but His own very Presence through the Holy Spirit.

The Doctrine of the Ministry enunciates this reality of the Holy Spirit, and the full necessity of His offices for the divine purposes in and through the Church. The Ministry itself, on its foundation as the Church's Ministry, is a continuing witness to the truth that there is this Resource in God for those called to be His servants; it is, we have seen, the Ministry's existence to be the channel of this Resource. What we have described as identity of function of the Ministry and the Holy Spirit enforces this quality of the Ministry: it is the priesthood of the Ministry to claim the Spirit for the Church, even as for itself. For it is by its knowledge of the Spirit's power, and its devotion to the ends for which the Church receives this power, that it stands or falls as truly the Christian Ministry.

Thus "The Ministry and the Holy Spirit," the theme of this section, lies near the pinnacle of our Doctrine of the Ministry and, if one heading can, compasses its substance. We speak of the Church as the Body of Christ: Christ, Himself invisible, is through the Church visibly active in the world. But the Spirit we have said chooses and consecrates a medium for *His* vocation; He too needs an organ for His testimony to men and activity in their behalf. By what our study has shown of community of function of the Spirit and the Ministry, the Ministry answers to this organ and could be named the Body or Visibility of the Holy Spirit.

We must not over-strain these parallels: Christ: the Church; the Holy Spirit : the Ministry. The Spirit is for the Church no less than for the Ministry; and as has been axiomatic for us all along, Christ 'sent' the Ministry even as He created the Church. Yet the relation of the Ministry and the Holy Spirit is crucial; it is for the Ministry constitutive and all-determining. The heart of Ordination to the Ministry is the bestowal of the Holy Spirit; by His giving of the Spirit Christ Himself instituted Ordination after the Resurrection (Lk. 24: 49; John 20: 21-23; Acts 1: 4-8). Pentecost was the descent of the Spirit to the whole assembled company that had been admonished to wait in Jerusalem for it; we can without undue forcing of phrase regard Pentecost as the Ordination of the Church. But no conjunction is closer than that of the Spirit and the Ministry; the Holy Spirit is the being of the Ministry, its life and energy and wisdom for its task; a task that cannot be fulfilled or even entered upon without the Spirit. The Spirit is not for the Ministry only; He "is given to every man to profit withal" (I Cor. 12 : 7). But there are "diversities of gifts as of administrations" (vv. 4, 5); for the Minister the special "gift of Ministry," the coming of the Spirit in singular fulness for his special calling. No hymnprayer anywhere is more fittingly in place than in the Service of Ordination to the Ministry:

> Come, Holy Ghost, our souls inspire,
> And lighten with celestial fire;
> Thou the anointing Spirit art . . .

III

The Ministry and the Church

We stated earlier in this chapter our thought of the Ministry as, while within and for the Church, not existing solely through it, but having its origin even as the Church in the purpose of God and bearing its own divinely-enjoined commission. The Minister's Word and Charge have immediate warrant from "the counsel that standeth sure."

But it was said too that being of divine authorization does not give the Ministry caste status or right of privilege. The Ministry is set apart for service; in one of its essential aspects it is the Servant of the Church, chosen and appointed by it. The Minister is endued with authority for this service, for leading the Church in its confession, worship and work. We shall now consider the Minister's office in the Church with these two dividing our thought:

the Minister's Service to the Church; the Minister's Authority within the Church.

a. The Minister's Service to the Church

It is often said in loose language that the Minister is a priest, in that it belongs to him, in his preaching and other ministration, to mediate to the people the things of God and to lead and help their approach to God. There is truth in this; but we shall give 'priest' here its particular usage by which to think of the Minister as priest is to attribute to him miraculously given power for this mediation. In possessing this power he is the definitive and sure Instrument for effecting that encounter of the soul with God and His gracious benefits on which its salvation depends. There are familiar doctrines of the Ministry that assert in essentially this way the priesthood of the Minister.

This is a view of the Ministry for which the New Testament offers little ready support. Christian Ministers are not named 'priests' (ἱερεύς) in the New Testament, save as they are included with Christians generally who are all "kings and priests" (Rev. 1: 6) or corporately "a royal priesthood" (I Peter 2: 9). Christians had no general aversion to Jewish titles; they adopt 'elder' and use it freely of their principal local Church officers. The avoidance of 'priest' could then have been deliberate; Christians felt that the functions of their Ministers were not priestly after the manner of Jewish priests. They had one priest, a High Priest for ever, the Lord Himself, but He was Minister of the true tabernacle (Heb. 8: 2), His priesthood not the changing one of the cultus but of the order of Melchizedek (7: 21-24). Attempts have been made to find a nascent Christian priesthood in those of Acts 13: 1, 2 who "ministered unto the Lord," the form from Aaron onward (Ex. 28: 1) for the service or 'liturgy' of priests. The persons spoken of, however, in Acts 13 are prophets. There were Jewish priests who had joined the Christian company (Acts 6: 7); these may have become prophets, and "ministering unto the Lord" may signalize their continuing as prophets the more spiritual phases of their calling as priests.

In the period following the New Testament a change is noticeable; the practice has begun of referring to Christian Ministers as priests. An instance is in the *Didache*, a writing variously assigned to the late first century or to dates well into the second; and we may deem it of note, in view of what we have just seen of 'ministering' by prophets in Acts 13, that it is prophets in the *Didache* who are called 'priests' or even 'high priests,'[1] the Eucharist conformably to this being in the near context called a 'sacrifice'.[2] These terms may retain here chiefly their spiritual meaning, as in the New Testament when Paul exhorts his readers to 'sacrifice' (Rom. 12 : 1) and the author of the Book of Revelation calls believers 'priests' (1 : 6). But more formal Christian priestly developments are on the horizon and must have our thought, since our present question whether the Minister is a priest may depend considerably on our adjudgment of them.

We remarked earlier on the possibility of reading back from later trends in the Church to discern in the light of these, in New Testament Church life, features otherwise hidden, whence may have come these trends and many of the further transformations in Church order which history would record. It is this procedure that discovers an early phase of Christian priesthood in the "ministering unto the Lord" of Acts 13 : 2. But over against this was our alternative suggestion of possible departures from New Testament ways in the age when as yet the Church lacked the authoritative general directive she would eventually have in the commonly received New Testament books. We applied this counter-possibility in considering the Catholic conception of Episcopacy which came to birth in this age. Now at this stage we can look to it for light on the problem of the growth and character of priesthood in the Church.

Its bearing on this problem could be after this wise: Jewish Christians in participating with others in an emerging Christian cultus would naturally bring to it leading

[1] XIII.   [2] XIV.

elements from their Jewish training; in particular, the destruction in A.D. 70 of the Temple priesthood and worship leaving a breach for Jews and Jewish Christians alike (Acts 3: 1), the latter, as Jews long inured to the institute of priesthood, could have sought recompense in giving title and some of the duties of priest to Christian Ministers. Or particular Christian Ministries may have seemed the proper residuary of Priesthood and High Priesthood, now fallen from Jewish hands. This would return us for the roots of the Church's special priesthood to the Jewish hierarchic order, in place of supposing for it an implicit New Testament origin; and it would accord with what we have seen of the influence, before the New Testament could be formed as Scripture, of Old Testament-Jewish thought and practice in the post-Apostolic Church.

These trends toward a priestly ideal of the Ministry were helped by another change the age was witnessing, and which was occurring largely from the same negative cause: the absence of general use of or dependence upon the New Testament writings. This change lay in a far-reaching alteration in the Church's teaching concerning Grace *(χάρις)*. Grace in the New Testament, in the dominant conception of it, is God's act and gift in providing redemption for the sinful world, in proffering justification and forgiveness, not to compensate our achievement but as His bounty to the undeserving. But, with the New Testament belief slipping from the Church's grasp, Grace acquired other meanings under influences from the Jewish legal outlook as partially being resumed in the Church, and still more from Hellenistic thought habits as Christianity spread in the non-Palestinian world. Grace became a force or quality divinely afforded, not for a salvation that must ever remain unmerited, but for the perfecting of self-endeavour toward the holy state in the attainment of which salvation lay. It was thus "related to the continuance of the Christian life, rather than to the decisive motion of God's love as the presupposition of the whole Christian life."[1]

This turn in the thinking about Grace was the fore-

[1] Torrance, *The Doctrine of Grace in the Apostolic Fathers*, p. 139.

141

runner of the *gratia infusa* of the Church's later order; but we do not have to wait for this before discerning the implications of this changed notion of Grace for the matter now before us, the beginnings of the priestly Ministry. For already in this primary phase where Grace is no longer the prevenient divine gift but is given of God currently for Christian perseverance, the call would be for ways and forms for mediating this Grace or specifically for its divinely-authenticated medium in priesthood and priestly ordinance. It is thus that the transition to a priestly view of the Ministry was effectually aided by these changes in the Church's conception of Grace.

Dr. Kirk, who nevertheless favours many of the trends toward Catholic order that emerged in the post-Apostolic period, is alive to the doctrinal import of these movements of the Church's thought and is frank concerning their character as a lapse from New Testament principles.

> The primary evangelical feature of Redeeming Grace [he writes] had fallen into the background, altering the whole balance of New Testament theology . . . St. Paul's indignant wonder was evoked by the reversion of a small province of the Christian Church to the legalist spirit of the Jewish religion. Had he lived half a century later, his cause for amazement would have been increased a hundredfold . . . writer after writer seems to have little other interest than to express the genius of Christianity wholly in terms of law and obedience.[1]

These are strong words, and they clearly lay upon us that for standards in judging what Christian beliefs about redemption, law and grace truly are we must repair to Christianity as authentically given in the New Testament prior to this declension in the representation of it. Our present interest, however, turns on the possibility of an equal result for our own subject. For we have intimated a close interrelation of these departures in doctrine, the dearth of New Testament understanding that underlay them, and changing ideas and attitudes pertaining to the

[1] *The Vision of God*, p. 111.

Ministry. This interrelation carries the presumption for us very near to certainty that what is normative for the Ministry is also to be had in its New Testament forms.

We return, then, to these, still asking: Do we meet among them any signs of a priestly ordinance of Ministry or of Ministers fulfilling distinctly priestly acts? We noted the negative circumstance: Ministers are not called priests. This we feel ought not to be reckoned inconsiderable; but the issue is not resolved by it alone.

A pertinent study is Heb. 8: 1 ff., a portion of which we transcribe:

> We have such an high priest, who is set on the right hand of the throne of the Majesty in the heavens;
> A minister of the sanctuary, and of the true tabernacle, which the Lord pitched, and not man.
> For every high priest is ordained to offer gifts and sacrifices; wherefore it is of necessity that this man have somewhat also to offer.

Christ is here presented as offering sacrifices in the heavenly temple. Does this mean that His self-offering was not completed on Calvary: there He *made* the oblation, but He still brings and offers it to God on high? Yet given this as so, it would not make Ministers on earth to be priests and offerers of sacrifice. But note the result of adding to this in Hebrews, the words of Paul in Rom. 15: 16: " That I should be the minister of Jesus Christ to the Gentiles, ministering [ἱερουργέω: to minister in holy things] the Gospel of God, that the offering up of the Gentiles might be acceptable." Here let us not omit to note, if the noun (ἱερεύς : priest) is never applied to New Testament Ministers, Paul does use the cognate verbal form referring to his own office. Hebert's comment is: " St. Paul represents himself as a sacrificing priest, the Gentiles as a sacrificial offering to God."[1] Further, in Rom. 12: 1, Paul entreats his readers to present their bodies to God, a living, holy sacrifice.

These and other allusions in the New Testament to

[1] *Liturgy and Society*, p. 80.

Christian offering of sacrifice have, taken together, been held favourable to the thought of the Church or the Ministry as united to Christ in His devotion and called to share His continuing sacrifice. As His offering in the heavens is His body ("a body hast thou prepared me . . . Lo, I come to do thy will, O God": Heb. 10: 5, 7), so the Church on earth offers His Body in the consecrated eucharistic elements. The sacrifice of the Head is completed in that of His members; the Church makes an oblation that has its ground in Christ's oblation and derives its fulness from it. There is a grandeur in this that is strange and appealing; embodied in the Catholic doctrine of the Sacrifice of the Mass, it gives to that doctrine as to the rite itself its fascinating and powerfully moving numinous quality. Or in another view, the thought of continuing sacrifice opens to us a still sublimer vision: sacrifice is ever being offered, the whole spiritual-universal order is an order of redemption for the renewal of man by redemptive sacrifice. And for such an order, for salvation within it, must there not be a Ministry priestly in function and enduement: a priesthood for the sacrifice?

Yet for all its impressiveness and might of appeal, I cannot feel that doctrinally this case for Christian eucharistic sacrifice or sacerdotal priesthood rests on stable assumptions. The passage given above from Hebrews (8: 1 ff.) may seem patient by itself of the interpretation which makes it tell of continuing or repeated sacrifice; but kept to its setting within the Epistle, it bears almost the opposite meaning: not that Christ now makes or offers a sacrifice, but He brings one to the heavenly altar that is wholly acceptable precisely on the ground that already it has been made and perfected. For just this is an emphatic theme of the Epistle: the all-sufficiency of the One Sacrifice completed in the One Offering. Heed as evidence some of its expressions: "Christ was once offered to bear the sins of many" (9: 28); "we are sanctified through the offering of the body of Jesus Christ once for all" (10: 10); "after He had offered one sacrifice for sins for ever, He sat down at the right hand of God" (v. 12). We sing and exhort, "*Rise up*

ye men of God," our work still to be done; what figure
could be more eloquent of His accomplished work than
that He *sat down* with God? This connection of Christ's
heavenly 'session' and His completed work is made most
succinctly in 1 : 3: "when He had by Himself purged our
sins, He sat down at the right hand of the Majesty on high."
It would be hard to excel the verbal economy of " He *had*
by *Himself*" for the two notions of the Sacrifice as *fait
accompli* and as His alone.

Further to this issue, it is on Christ's once-fulfilled Sacrifice making other sacrifices unnecessary that this writer
hangs his whole comparison of the older priesthood and
sacrifice and Christ's High Priesthood: " He needs not
daily, as those other priests, to offer sacrifice, for this He did
once when He offered up Himself" (7: 27). So the ordeal
is past; Christ has 'endured' the Cross and is *now* at God's
right hand (12: 2); His suffering obedience unto death was
full obedience, perfecting even Himself as well as the salvation He brought (5: 7-9). For Him remain the past and
perfect but no present tense in the grammar of propitiatory
sacrifice. The Church sings this Deed accomplished in
" The strife is *o'er*" and other anthems to it in her common
praise.

Nevertheless there is left to Christ a heavenly offering,
not piacular but intercessory: " He is able to save to the
uttermost, seeing He ever liveth to make intercession " (7:
25). The Reconciler having wrought the Reconciliation is
' seated' on high, not in honorary dignity as the ex-Recon-
ciler, but in authority at the right hand of God to work out
His reconciliation through the course of history, or as the
perpetual providence of His own salvation working through
His Spirit, to administer and apply the exhaustless energy
of His Saving Act in the actual restoring of men to God.
This is an offering, Christ's saving ministry of intercession,
that we on earth can share, though here too we are first
indebted to it and dependent upon it. But returning to the
redemptive sacrifice, it seems certain from what was shown
above that the text in Hebrews which some regard as implying Christ's continuing oblationary sacrifice is within a

writing that extols His "full, perfect and sufficient" work and sacrifice almost more than any other New Testament book. Hence we cannot rest on these words in Hebrews the conception of the Ministry as priestly in being partner with Christ in an ever-renewed altar sacrifice and self-offering to God.

What, then, of our other reference where Paul speaks of himself as offering sacrifice and urges such offering upon his readers? Here again the thought is not of piacular sacrifice, but on the one hand of personal consecration leading to singleness of mind in God's service (Rom. 12: 1), and on the other of presenting to God the fruits of that service (15: 16). This truly is a discipline of sacrifice: the offering of ourselves and of our works to God as Paul offers his winning of the Gentiles, not for merit or reward, but as being 'acceptable' to Him and His due in their having come through His working in us, so in their essence "not unto us but unto Him." But such sacrifice is for all Christians, not the specialty of a sacerdotal Ministry, and enriches and fulfils all Christian service.

This, however, is not the whole of the Church's offering of sacrifice. God does not ask to be placated or cajoled; but neither is the sacrifice we bring to Him in "presenting our bodies" purely an ethical act, our resolve and pledge to make His will our rule of life. There is offering to Him of a deeper order. The words of Jesus at the Last Supper, This is my Body, if we take account of His Aramaic speech could perhaps be rendered, This is my Self; their force would then bear His pledge to His disciples that His death, now imminent, would be as had been His life, one of self-sacrifice for them. His sacrifice in death was not the mere formal or ritual "shedding of blood," but the total giving up of Himself, of His soul or life ($\psi v \chi \eta$: Mk. 10: 45), that the 'many' might be ransomed from sin and "made righteous" (Rom. 5: 19). But this end is not yet attained; the 'many' are not made righteous and sin still abounds. Whence Christ still offers Himself to us and to God for us, for our reconciliation to Him; this offering of Himself blends in one His ministries of reconciliation and intercession, and

146

continuing while the need for it remains is truly a perpetual sacrifice, not propitiatory but of His steadfastness and purpose to complete for our sake the work He has begun. And by the union of the Church with Christ, the Church participates in this self-offering. For the Church too is not for itself, but gives itself and in its unity with Christ gives or offers Him; offers Him to a sinful world and as the instrument of His mediation and reconciliation bears the world up before God in prayer and devout dedication.

This devotion of the Church reaches the height in the sacramental consecration, where the Church is " doing in remembrance " as Christ commanded and "showing forth the Lord's death." This " showing forth " of the Lord's sacrifice if more than formal connotes some sharing by the Church of Christ's sacrificial vocation, though with its members it must still have its being by it and live of its benefits. But this sharing again is not exclusive to the Ministry; it is not the offering of sacrifice by a priestly order. The Minister is the organ of the Church's own " royal priesthood," and in his sacramental as in his other offices acts for the Church, even while being just as truly the voice and vehicle of what " the Spirit saith " to the Church.

We have been considering in these paragraphs the priestly conception of the Ministry; taking a look at the New Testament texts that have been "inquired of" for support of this conception, and setting down certain of our own thoughts on the manner in which Church and Ministry may have part with Christ in His sacrificial work. It remains to stress that nothing we have said touches the basic truth that the real decisiveness of Christ's sacrificial offering is singularly His own. For the offering of Christ by Church or Minister is offering by, and of, another, where the virtue, cruciality and efficacy of Christ's act lay in its being His *Self*-offering (" when He had by *Himself* purged our sins ": "this He did once when He offered up *Himself*": Heb. 1: 3; 7: 27).

This difference holds, however we conceive the Church being the Body of Christ to involve identification of the Church and Christ. For in such blendings into one, unity can reach to the full whole of interchangeability; but always if it is union, not obliteration, of identities, there is residual to each participant what is not interchangeable, the irreplaceable core of *self*-being. It is this depth and centre of the being of Christ whence comes His sacrificial offering as Self-offering. For in His essential Self, as well as being one with us Christ is separate from us: separate from sinners (Heb. 7: 26), and because of this free to take their sin upon Him and save to the uttermost. He was "made sin for us, who knew no sin." His separateness from sinners qualifies His sacrifice for them as also separate, not the work of one who was himself "compassed with infirmity"; and it has constrained the Church in her doctrine to own in the Work of Christ a character as unsharable as the essence of His Person. "There was none other good enough, to pay the price of sin." The result to which this leads is that whatever the bond uniting Ministry and Church to Christ, whatever by reason of this bond Church or Ministry may bring of sacrificial offering, the Self-offering which is the prevailing energy and sufficiency of the saving institute is of Christ's perfection and for His one oblation; an oblation made complete when His yielding to death proved the path to His triumph over it.

The issue of this part of our discussion as it affects our question would thus appear to point away from the special sacerdotal Ministry. If we link to it our findings in other parts of this work, especially what has seemed to us the general tenor of the New Testament on the subject of the Ministry, our conclusion will ripen: the Minister as shaped by the forces that begat him and as in the Apostolic and early Church he "made proof of his Ministry" (2 Tim. 4: 5) is not a hierarchic altar priest but, as we are naming him in this section, a servant of the Gospel Word and of the Church begotten of the Word. We can here weave positively into our Doctrine the fact of 'to serve' (διακονέω) being appropriate to all Ministries, noted earlier[1] in its negative suggestiveness regarding the Seven of Acts 6 and the Diaconate. As servant of the Church the Minister's voca-

[1] *supra*, p. 76.

tion is high: he ministers the Word to the Church in teaching and ordinance and, as commissioned by her, prays, acts and labours in her behalf. This meaning of the Ministry the Church has never lost or wholly relinquished; amid the extremest developments of sacerdotal theory and claims to authority, the belief has survived that the Ministry is for the Church and exists by sanction of it. If God, as we have asseverated, is first in the making of a Minister, the Church is second, in that the Church chooses and prepares her own servants, the Holy Spirit guiding her choice. The Ministry's genesis is in God, but the Church is its matrix and habitat; it is, with all who receive the Word, born of God, not of the will of the flesh (John 1: 13), but it is confirmed and nurtured within the Church.

This is the Biblical order. The Seven of Acts 6 were men full of the Holy Ghost: God had first acted. But they were still to be chosen till the Church chose; "choose from among you" the Apostles ask the company (v. 3). Though from those God had already chosen, it was real choice by the Church. So it continued in the New Testament. In Acts 13: 2, 3, Barnabas and Saul are first the Holy Spirit's choice, then at His instance they are separated and ordained by the Church. The instructions regarding bishops and deacons in the Pastoral Epistles clearly enjoin choice and ordainment by Timothy, Titus and others; but the qualifications required in those to be ordained (I Tim. 3: 1 ff.; Titus 1: 5 ff.) make it just as clear that God's work has already been begun and is progressing in them. After being ordained by Apostle (I Tim. 1: 3) or presbytery (4: 14) Ministers are still approved unto God by diligent and faithful service to the Church (2 Tim. 2: 15).

This order has remained to the Church in principle, and to a wide degree in formal practice. The Ministry throughout the Church's history, arising out of the will and at the command of God, has been authorized with the consent of the Church or has been presented to the Church for confirmation at its hands. This confirmation by the Church early became embodied in the rite or sacrament of Ordination; the two acts in Ordination, prayer and the laying on of hands, are acts of the Church or of Ministers carrying out the will of the Church. But they are done when the Church and its leaders are persuaded that God has been before them in calling and claiming those on whom their hands will be laid, and that He will grant them the Spirit for Ministry besought by the Church's prayer.

The instances of Acts 6 and 13 are the exemplar for the Christian ages of the creation of Ministry as first ordained of God, then set apart to be fulfilled in the service of the Church. Other parts of the New Testament, the Pastoral Epistles, I Peter, John ch. 15, I Cor. chs. 3, 12, Eph. chs. 3, 4 and other texts in Paul, fill out this portrait of the Ministry. It is Ministry elected of God, not to be imposed on the Church for lordly rule (I Peter 5: 3), but given to and accepted by it to feed the flock and to be the Church's voice in proclaiming the Kingdom to men. The Ministry is the servant of all in being the servant of the Church.

b. *The Minister's Authority within the Church*

Jesus gave authority to His Ministers (Lk. 9: 1); His own authority, than which none can be higher. Such a gift was fraught with danger. Who "the heir of man's infirmities" can hold such authority and not feel inducted by it into ascendency and rule?

The Minister's cross has always been to constrain into one his authority and fidelity to his vocation of service. His existence battles with a contradiction that is resolved only in rare moments of self-dedication. In those moments he knows, not how to reconcile authority and service, but the deeper secret that removes the need for this reconciliation in the discernment that only in service can he in Christian loyalty possess his authority. This comes of his authority being Christ's own, who was "among us as he that serveth" (Lk. 22: 27).

When authority slips from this, it descends the slope to the authoritarian, its own false image. There are authoritarian individuals as well as states; authoritarian Ministers as well as Churches. Authoritarianism is not undue assertion of proper authority, but its perversion and counterfeit; it is arbitrary assumption of 'authority' by sheer power to mask the absence or failure of responsible authority. It is the devil's obverse of the ἐξουσία which Jesus bestowed.

It will help our consideration of the Minister's authority, to distinguish Catholic and Reformed Church conceptions of it.

In the Catholic view, the Minister is Priest at the altar, where the miracle is wrought whereby Christ becomes present corporeally to be offered in sacrifice and in His real Body dispensed to His faithful people. The Minister's power for this miracle clothes him with authority at the place where the thing is done on which man's salvation depends. This power was first exercised by Christ at the Supper in the upper room in the act by which He gave bread with the words, "This is my Body"; adding immediately "this do ye" (Lk. 22: 19), to give to His Ministers the selfsame power.

In the Reformed or Evangelical view, the Minister is Minister of the Word. He proclaims the Gospel and, by the same authority under which he does this, administers the sacraments in the congregation. This authority is not something external or superadded to his preaching of the Word; it is the Word's own authority. The Minister is given power to proclaim the Gospel in being called to do it; his authority is intrinsic to this gift and to the call. It is what he inwardly receives and possesses in becoming Minister. This is what we found earlier in another expression: one is both made Minister and empowered for Ministry through the coming of the Spirit. In like manner Jesus gave authority to His Ministers with His call to them and His sending them forth (Lk. 9: 1, 2).

If I want to teach mathematics, I sit at the feet of a master and receive (learn) from him. Then with what I have I teach. My authority to teach is not aside from what I have received, a bonus from without; in receiving the mathematics, the knowledge, I have therein what enables my teaching, gives authority to it. An official group may engage me, but my power as I teach is my grasp of the subject. So

Jesus said, Go teach (Mt. 28: 19) to those who had learned of Him (11: 29).

Save for this great difference. The thing we learn of Jesus, possess through Him, is not formal intellectual knowledge, as in the learner of mathematics; but truth for the renewal of our being, our sanctification and victory over evil. The power or authority had by this is not the right to teach through objective familiarity in the field of the teaching; it is power and authority from total life-appropriation of what Christ has imparted, with all one's values, ends and hopes re-fashioned to the quality of it. "Learn of me," He says, not to accumulate a stock of transmissible understanding, but that "ye may find rest unto your souls."

This may seem to conflict with a principle that has generally commended itself to Church historians: the principle that the validity of the Gospel ordinances does not depend on the character or spiritual state of the official ministrant of them. This principle it is necessary to uphold. It is not as God would dispose that people, seeking fresh assurance of His saving benefits through Mass or Sacrament or the Word preached to them, should be at the mercy of the fallible human instrument. If the *people* are sincere and truly seek, God is not debarred by unworthiness in another from honouring His promise that they who seek shall find.

But this does not imply that the personal attitude of the Minister, in the pulpit or at the altar, is of no consequence. Certainly it helps the people if they have confidence that the Minister's sincerity is joined with their own. But beyond this, by what we have said of personal appropriation being the proper response to what Christ gives, and of power and authority in the Minister being reinforced by this appropriation, it becomes essential—at least to fulness of efficacy in preaching the Word—that the authority of the Word itself be confirmed by this other that is personal to the Minister in being one with *his* possession of the Word. "If my words abide in *you*," said Jesus, "ye shall ask what ye will . . . The branch cannot bear fruit except it abide in the vine" (John 15: 4, 7). Something, then, does depend on the spiritual integrity of the Minister, on his abiding in the

Vine. Not abiding, by this word of Jesus his Ministry is without fruit. So while the validity or efficacy of sacraments is not made or unmade by Priest's or Minister's intention —God does not because of defect in that intention withhold His grace from devout suppliants—there are other ranges of the Minister's influence and spiritual outcome of his endeavours wherein it does rest with him to make or mar. Here the decision for an efficacious (in Jesus' word, fruit-bearing) Ministry is crucially the Minister's; his authority gives its measure to his responsibility.

The Minister called of God can, under this new sign, forget authority. Authority we have stressed is assured with the call; hence, given the call, is not in doubt. But he will have in constant regard the responsibility which the authority implies, and demands if it is to be effectual toward the divine ends for which it is given.

We shall consider this demand still within the reference of Catholic and Reformed conceptions of the Ministry. By what rule can we compare what is demanded of the Minister who is priest at the altar and the requirements laid upon him as Minister of the Word?

It is easily supposed that Catholic ideas of ministerial order and function give the Minister's work a quality of necessity and arm him with prerogatives that are higher than any he assumes or claims under the Protestant belief. The Priest under the Catholic rubric presides at a miracle through which the consecration of the sacramental elements becomes their conversion into Christ's actual being, to the certification of His Presence to the assembled people in the mode wholly consonant to their spiritual needs. The Reformed Church Minister's offices are simpler and can seem more commonplace; he preaches the Gospel and administers the sacraments as the Reformed Churches receive them, but is not empowered to "bring Christ down" to be present at the sacrament. He believes Christ is present at His table, but not through a metaphysical miracle he himself performs; His presence is through the Holy Spirit who, as Christ's redeeming sacrifice is remembered, makes real its benefits unto salvation and holiness, to those who respond in faith and with purpose to lead more earnestly "the new life, following the commands of God."

The Priest, then, receives and exercises a special divine gift the Minister does not share, the gift of power for this deed of transubstantiation, for changing the bread and wine on the sacramental altar into Christ's substantial Body and Blood. This power, as we have already noted, Christ gave His priests at the Last Supper: first, the power being His own, He employed it to make effectual the words "This is my Body" in dispensing the bread; then with the behest "This do," He imparted the power to the Apostles. The Protestant Minister asks no such power or supranatural conferment; enough for him the graces and gifts for his calling as Minister of the Word. The Priest requires for his 'liturgy' vaster divine enduements than the Minister either expects or needs.

But pause a moment. The belief in transubstantiation does postulate a miraculous happening; *preaching*, though helped by the Holy Spirit, may seem picturable as a human act in a natural setting. But what is the assumption of preaching? Just this: the Holy Spirit takes the utterance of the preacher, which as emanating from him carries its quota of human frailty, and makes it the vehicle of the Word of God or receivable as the Word by the preacher's hearers.

What pertinence has preaching to its objective, how is it Preaching the Word, if this is not so? Now let the preacher recall his thrusts and retreats in preparing a sermon, how feeble he feels his effort when he is delivering it, and then consider: if that is convertible into the Word of God, does it not imply supernatural working as truly as anything priesthood may effect at Eucharist or Mass? To transform bread and wine into the Body and Blood; to take one's faltering speech and render it as the Word: which is the greater miracle? Save that the latter, in the realm not of ritual externals but of inner apprehension and appropriation of divine truth in preacher and hearer, is more consonant with the Holy Spirit's proper activity and with the end for which He was given. That the Spirit would guide into truth and show divine things to men is the New Testament assurance; even just those things that are 'hidden' as humanly uttered till revealed by the Spirit (John 16: 13, 14; I Cor. 2: 7-10). The Spirit speaking in the word of those who trust to Him is expressly promised (Mt. 10: 20). When the Spirit, then, leads men to the Gospel in the word they hear; when human speech becomes the voice of the Spirit; things are happening precisely as the New Testament said.

Thus it is that what the Protestant expects of the Spirit through the Gospel ministration is not only a divine work as surely as what the Catholic looks for in the Eucharist, but it is in straight accord with what Jesus and others in the Scriptures foretold and knew through the coming of the Spirit. We know no equal Scriptural attestation of the Catholic form of transubstantiation as God's central means for bestowing upon men His saving grace. There is truth to transubstantiation, but, as the New Testament knows it, it is not in the field of subsistence, material or metaphysical. In the sacrament it is the Holy Spirit's operation whereby Christ's people receiving the " creatures of bread and wine " are assured of His presence to them. It is instanced again in this other of which we are thinking, the translating of the preacher's human word into the *substance*, the very reality, of the divine Gospel. This is miracle at which the Minister may surely wonder, the more that he has been elected for God's fulfilment of it.

In the light of this, it can no longer appear as beyond question that the Priesthood is a more highly endued order of Ministry, with higher authority, than the Evangelical Ministry. The call to Ministry is the call to mediate God's redemption, and for all Ministries it is one call. There is no *sacerdotium* for the Ministry of the altar that surpasses that of the Ministry of the Word, if it is as we maintain that the word of the preacher becoming God's Word is God's marvellous doing no less than what is done at the altar, and if divine redemption reaches men through the Word. In one regard the Reformed Church doctrine of the

Ministry exceeds the Catholic: in what it requires in the person of the Minister. The Priest's supreme office is a ritual act where, as is allowed or even asserted, the character of the officiant is not determining; suffice it that he do faithfully as the Church authorizes and appoints. But we found it of the Evangelical Minister's vocation to match authority with responsibility; a work falls to him that turns to nullity " except *he* abide in the Vine."

The Protestant standard for the Ministry would seem by this to be higher than the Catholic in what it exacts of the Minister himself. It is not enough that he be in valid Orders; he must personally and in his own purpose be joined to Christ and know his dependence on the Holy Spirit. This is the burden of the Evangelical Minister: his being in his place not by ordinance of the Church only, but in personal liability and committed involvement in all for which the Church stands and which he as its Minister in Word and Sacrament professes and administers. Being servant of the Word claims the Minister existentially, and tests more crucially his readiness himself to 'drink of the cup " (Mk. 10: 38, 39) than being Priest at the altar is wont to do; save that Priest too can be Minister of the Word: this Ministry then in him claims his full service and is excelled by no other he is called to fulfil.

But it will be felt by some that our comparison of Catholic and Protestant Ministries so far as it has gone has left out a main element: the Priest's power of absolution. Does not this power robe Priesthood with a quality of office and authority beyond anything attributable to the Ministry? This question affords the opportunity to state— appropriately to this section on authority—such thought as we have on the subject of the keys (Mt. 16: 19), the charge given to the Apostles to remit and retain sins (John 20: 23).

It will help in this if first we disburden 'remission' or 'forgiveness' of undue legal connotation, and give it its evangelical and ethical force. The word "to forgive" (ἀφίημι) in the New Testament means among other things "to send away "; it is used of a man sending away or divorcing his wife (I Cor. 7: 11). Forgiveness of sins, then, is sending one's sins from him, releasing or separating him from them. The force of this is inclusive. Jesus came to "save His people from their sins," not from the penalty of sin or its guilt apart from "taking or bearing away" the sin itself. Salvation from sin covers, in one, the sin, its guilt and power. He is without fear and "cometh not into condemnation" who has been 'loosed' from his sin.

But God sent His Son and has given His Word for this very end, that men may be freed from their sin. Their sin separates men from Him; forgiveness, the separating of men from that which separates from Him, is their reconciliation to Him. Forgiveness and reconciliation are negative and positive of the one divine work to end man's entanglement with sin and restore the communion of man and God that sin had destroyed.

The Minister who is servant of the Word declares and seeks to make effectual this forgiveness and reconciliation. He bears forgiveness of sins to men in offering the forgiving and reconciling Word and in being faithful to it. But what if he be unfaithful, wrest or withhold this Word? Does he not then by equal implication, in exercising his office thus unworthily, serve toward the retaining of sins? The power of the Keys, to forgive or retain sins, is no arbitrary enduement but the power of the man entrusted with God's forgiving Word, which he may apply to the saving of his hearers or use vainly to the subverting of them (2 Tim. 2: 14). This is confirmed when Jesus speaks of those who take away the key of knowledge and keep others from entering the Kingdom (Lk. 11: 52). They do this not by misemploying some extrinsic function but by being false to their calling as the people's teachers and guides. The knowledge unfaithful teachers 'take away' is for Christians God's Word of grace in Jesus Christ; this it is that offers entrance to the Kingdom. Christ gives the "keys of the Kingdom" (Mt. 16: 19) in giving this Word. Thus the lesson of the keys is the solemnity of the charge laid upon the Minister as ambassador of the Word and the decisiveness of his authority. This authority has this decisiveness in being, as we have seen, Christ's own (Lk. 9: 1), who exercised it also in teaching the Word (Mt. 7: 29: "He *taught* as one having authority").

Here is one ground of Christ's assurance, accompanying the gift of the Keys, that "binding and loosing" in heaven will ratify the Minister's "binding and loosing" (Mt. 16: 19; John 20: 23): both are subject to the one authority (Mt. 28: 18). Another basis is this: "binding and loosing" (retaining and remitting sins) hanging as we have been saying on man's response to the forgiving Word, the fact of this being one Word in Christ who brings and in Ministers who bear it carries the pledge of Christ's acceptance on high of the earthly acts of His faithful Ministers. Put another way, the testimony of Ministers as prophets of the Word to what is lawful and unlawful by Kingdom standards is sure of divine validation through the divine authority with which they are endued and the Spirit's guidance of them. Not that they have this authority infallibly or that God's resources are spent in what He has given to them. He is not powerless if His Ministers falter; yet there is no weightier trust than the one He has committed to them, and the degree to which they *impede the Kingdom* by their betrayal of it is surpassed only by their *service to the Kingdom* if they keep the trust. The words in Mt. 16: 19 are a unique figuration of this; whence the deep things of the Ministry are in them, the crucial things for all to whom Ministry means "working together with God" in His "Ministry of reconciliation" (2 Cor. 5: 18) and who have in this allegiance their seal and rank as Ministers.

These two themes that have divided this section, the Minister servant of the Church and set in authority within it, distinguished for convenience of our discussion, are not apart from each other in the Minister's actual functioning. By declaring, under the authority given to him, God's will for the Church and for the world through the Church, the Minister equally serves the Church in continually relighting her vision and returning her to her task. Conversely, this and the Minister's other 'services' to the Church, of comfort, edification and counsel, have their full quality in being from one who comes not at his own charge but under the investiture of God. So are service and authority blent in one; "the chief or first is the servant of all" (Mk. 9: 35; Lk. 22: 26).

The Church needs today this fulness of Ministry: the Ministry for its service, to lead it to new life and hope and certainty of power; the authoritative prophetic Ministry, to rebuke and instruct and bring the Church to judgment, and to impel her to fresh adventurousness in realizing what is involved in being the Church, and in assuming unsparingly to herself and her institutional concerns the commitments and hazards of her world travail. It does not take Brunner's devastating word, that the Ecclesia of the New Testament is not that which the Church now is,[1] to open our eyes to disquieting contrasts between the Spirit-filled fellowship of the first chapters of *Acts* and what we now call our Churches, with their complexity of organization and so much that is sectional and secular in their interest and tone. The present condition of the Church calls aloud for Ministry with undoubted authority to declare to her "what the Spirit saith unto the Churches"; and with will and knowledge to serve her by securing to her that grasp of her world responsibility whereby she herself becomes God's arm of authority for, under the grace through which she serves, the present baffled age.

IV

The Continuing Ministry

We have affirmed in this work the divine basis of the Ministry, its Apostolic character and office, and have commended the doctrine of Apostolic Succession for the testimony it has borne to this. To our mind, its service in this way has been unique; for while certain other doctrines of the Ministry proceed from data or principles whence they derive the Ministry's divine quality, for Apostolic Succes-

[1] *The Misunderstanding of the Church*, p. 10.

sion this quality is the principle. Without it this doctrine could not have arisen.

But affirming the divine ground and the Apostolicity of the Ministry is not the only interest of Apostolic Succession. Another on which it places equal stress is its conception of the transmission of the Ministry down the path of history. We see this as calling for separate appraisal; since we can be agreed on the divine inception and gift of Ministry and still ask, Is this divine gift bestowed severally generation by generation or Minister by Minister as God calls and endues each? Or is it of God's method for the continuance of Ministry that the Ministry be, after its first institution, substantially engendered from previous Ministry, the powers descending from one to other that were initially divinely conferred?

It is self-evident that the Ministry must be continuing; Ministers are needed in one age as in another. Further, it has never been the Church's belief that the Ministry is a congeries of atomic units, God calling one, then another, by separate or discrete acts, the tie among Ministers being hardly more than temporal or vocational juxtaposition. The origination of the Ministry with God has not forbidden the other fact, to Church folk of common knowledge, that normally it is begotten within the Church, its spiritual parentage being not infrequently other Ministers.

It has been charged, however, that the Protestant doctrine of the Ministry—God calls each Minister personally and this rather than being in right Orders authenticates the Ministry—tends toward this atomizing of the body of Ministers; more than that, the Protestant belief annuls the consequence of the Incarnation whereby God inserted Himself within the historical stream, making it that His action in history is properly a continuum instead of occurring chiefly of sporadic intrusion. God's activity being of this immanent order is confirmed from the fact of the Holy Spirit through which history is inwardly charged with the divine dynamic operation, and is not just open to its descent upon it "at sundry times and in divers manners." Protestantism, it is contended, reverts from this; it resumes the

'sundry' and the occasional, after the model of philo-
sophical Occasionalism which makes divine instant-by-
instant interposition the cause of the correspondences of
thought and bodily action. So for Protestants is the calling
of Ministers, by single darts of inspiration, each reaching to
a particular person and laying on each several one God's
constraint to be His Minister. This dissolves God's "unrest-
ing, unhasting, silent as light" agency which would seem
the corollary in His course for maintaining the Ministry of
His having dwelt with us in the Word made flesh and of
His perpetual presence in the Holy Spirit.

This charge against Protestantism might stand if Protestants, in affirming God's initiative in bringing forth the
Ministry, did nothing more. But they hold as surely as
Catholics that while the Ministry is conceived of God, it
exists and is ever renewed within the Church according to
her need. Whence as well as God's naming of each Minister
there subsists within the Church a means for ensuring the
Succession of Ministry, and it is through this means that
God regularly mediates His will and call. The issue
between Protestant and Catholic is over the factors and
forces that constitute the means and thus determine the
course of the Succession.

We say God regularly works through this means; none
would claim that He does so invariably. Place must be
retained in our Doctrine for God's special designation
extending to some who would not be chosen by the Church
or by other Ministers, or even might not be known to them.
God seems always to have worked this dual way: establishing orderly process but reserving His freedom against His
own ordering, if only so could altered situations be made
amenable to His unchanging ends.

In the Old Testament, God employs the two methods in
giving a Ministry to His covenant people. The methods
correspond on the whole to the ordinances of Priest and
Prophet. Aaron's Ministry "in the priest's office" is the
ordered institute; his 'liturgy' falls to his sons, and is "a
statute for ever unto him and his seed after him" (Ex. 28:
1, 40, 41, 43). In contradistinction from this, Amos the

prophet boasts his standing outside the continuing order; he was *not* a prophet's son, but a herdman whom the Lord took and to whom He said, Go prophesy (Amos 7: 14, 15). In other instances of special call, God marked His choice from birth or even prior to it; Jeremiah was "ordained prophet, before I formed thee . . . before thou camest forth" (Jer. 1: 5). The two courses in the appointing of Ministers recur in the New Testament. Paul is Minister not by man but by the will of God (Gal. 1: 1) to the degree of Jeremiah in being "separated from his mother's womb" (v. 15); and his call on the road to Damascus was not his being set next in some Order the Church was establishing, but Christ's apprehension of His "chosen vessel" in the person of one whom the Church so far from favouring as a Minister feared as an enemy (Acts 9: 13-15). Paul exemplifies also, however, the other principle, not only in designating successors to himself and instructing them to make like provision for future Ministry (2 Tim. 2: 2); but in receiving for himself, along with direct divine authorization, the Church's imprimatur (Acts 9: 17, 18) and ordination at her hands (13: 1-3). So in Paul the two procedures blend to make a single Minister.

This is the tale of Ministry generally in the New Testament: Ministry of this double derivation, lying under prophetic charge straight from God, but apportioned to specific office by priestly consecration within the Church. The example in Acts 13: 1, 2 of *prophets* "ministering unto the Lord," the identifying clause for the work of *priest* (Ex. 28: 1), epitomizes this tale, and is symptomatic of the New Testament fulness of Ministry which has ended the dissociation of prophetic and priestly Ministries in a deeper and more spiritual understanding of them. They are united, that is, through the Holy Spirit; it was to make of these one Ministry that the Spirit was given. For it is of this gift that the individual is called and himself receives the Spirit; while that the Spirit was given to the Church to abide with her means just as certainly that the Church is a medium of the Spirit to those whom she chooses and sets apart. It is one Spirit, from God immediately and through the

Church; the Minister's double portion, as a prophet once prayed (2 Kings 2: 9). He was asking for both: for the Spirit, the divine donation to himself, but also for 'thy' Spirit, addressing another prophet. Himself commissioned to prophesy, he is succeeding also to one formerly commissioned, and desires to derive through his 'father' (v. 12) already clothed with it (I Kings 17: 1-5), the Spirit that is from God.

This double mantle is every Minister's to covet; it is necessary to each one for fulness of his Ministry. Each must stir up the divine gift in *him*, and read clear the title to minister secured to him by the gift; each must possess himself of the legacy from his forebears which assures to him a portion with the great and division of spoil with the strong. Both of these are essential; yet a discernible primacy of the first yields, we believe, our clue in this matter of Succession. No truth about the Ministry surpasses the one concerning God's power, which He never delegates, to choose for His service whom He will, whatever their place in the Church's esteem or in that of other Ministers. It is then the Church's wisdom to acknowledge those so chosen. Careful study of the Apostolic and other early Fathers establishes that this choice by God was their great concern; divine authorization was their first demand in a Minister, with Succession valued so far as certifying this. The bishop in Ignatius is exalted not as within a Succession but as standing in the place of God. Irenaeus leans hard on Succession but for the accessibility and purity of the divine Word he hopes for by it. Succession was familiar to him from the practice in Jewish and Christian metropolitan centres of keeping the priestly and episcopal succession lists. It was an instrument ready to hand for the ends Irenaeus and others sought. But it was not, in the Church's formative years, espoused for itself so much as for the way it helped men's confidence in the Ministry's divine ground and calling; in other words, this early interest in Succession upholds our present contention that the *first* essential of Ministry is not that it stand within a tradition of Ministry but that it arise of God's act. This yields an important conclusion of our study: By the standard of the creative phase of Christian history, being in rightful Succession may signalize the absolute authentication of a Minister but is not itself such; still less is this latter to be asserted of some one order or channel of Succession.

To contemplate the nature of Christianity is to make this self-evident. When Bishop Neill, as we observed earlier, doubts if he can reconcile the conception of Succession in the work, *The Apostolic Ministry*, with the Christian doctrine of God, he is using the sure test. For it is to the Christian doctrine of God that all questions of Succession and of the Ministry generally are ultimately referable. According to this doctrine, God offers to men salvation in His kingdom and commands that the offer be made known. For fulfilling this command Ministry is needed, but to require that it be of one mould, the Gospel of salvation to reach men through one prescribed formal medium, seems gratuitous; what matters, if the Truth but come to men and perform its work with them? That God is careful of the form or delimitation of the means for mediating His saving Word exacts a rethinking of God as He is conceived from seeing His real care and end—whence the Ministry at all— that men receive the Word. It is this that nurtures our gravest doubts of exclusive Episcopacy, the theory that the succession of bishops and of those who have their office through them is the one full Gospel Ministry. Our stone of stumbling is not the historical development and record of the episcopal Ministry, nor the reverence felt for this record which we readily share; but this special theory, what it presupposes in God and what would be the nature of Christianity if the theory were true. The theory transposes what is secondary or even external to a place with the essential as New Testament Christianity *dis*poses these, in our reading of it.

We stress again, however, that to say 'secondary' is not to say 'unimportant'. Succession is not the absolute for the validation of the Ministry; but few things are absolute, and that Succession is not one of them does not breach our other position that it has in the ordering of the Ministry an extremely vital part. It is impressive how Scripture consistently traces in the making of Ministry something from other Ministers; "I will take of the spirit which is upon thee and put it upon them" (Num. 11: 17) from one of our primal instances, shows power for Ministry even as divine enduement to be so derived. Exceptions but confirm this rule. Amos, and Paul in his initial call, were Ministers not by Succession but by God's direct summons. Theirs was Ministry of pure nature, divine fulness of Ministry without admixture. But they were at the stage of vast beginnings and can hardly typify God's general working in the appointing of Ministers, which as we are seeing is mediate as well as direct. The mediate phase brings in Succession and joins it to God's immediate action, to give to Ministry arising of the will of God for each Minister a unity from descent through history and from common life in the Church. The Minister first hears the divine call but enters into the heritage of Ministry in responding in the Church at his place within it. Succession—not down one close corridor but the whole historical sweep of Ministry and witness— thus becomes momentous both for Church and Ministry; it is the Church giving those *personally* called of God proof of their call in installing them with all others who have been so called in her *continuing* Ministry.

It is more than this; for this act of the Church is not the Church actualizing God's choice of Ministers independently of Him, as it were sealing this divine choice from the human side. Rather God is with the Church as in His own first calling of the Ministry, and through this activity of the Church works to actualize His own choice, to make it effectual for the Church and through the Church for the world. Or further still, in this act and ordinance by which the Church establishes in her Ministry those whom God has called, God Himself employs and sanctifies Transmission and Succession to the realizing of His own will that there be always in the Church, in unbroken continuance, an agency for ministering to men His gift in Jesus Christ and its gracious benefits. Thus the whole act by which Ministry is created is of Him, of His activity as we have said both direct and mediate; and it is in rightful order when men as they enter upon the Ministry relate their call as at His hand, and then are consecrated under the hand of those who, already fulfilling this Ministry, act also at His command.

This consecration by the Church, through her Ministers and others she may instruct, of those whom God has chosen and given to her, is the rite of Ordination. Our discussion has reached the place for stating more definitely than we have yet done our thought on this. Ordination witnesses to both of the above-named essentials in the establishing of the Ministry, to God's decision and call and to the Church's interest in Succession and continuing Ministry. This is evinced when the ordaining Minister, in behalf of the Church and from his place as Minister, bestows office on him on whom hands are being laid with the words, "Take thou authority . . .", which betoken at once God's charge to the ordinand, He being the fount of the Authority, and continuing Ministry in being addressed by one already a Minister.

To some Churches Ordination is a sacrament. Whatever our position on this, it is a sacramental Ministry to which the ordinand is ordained and a sacramental life to which he is pledged. Does anything occur at Ordination other than the observance of the form which marks the Church's acceptance of the ordinand for her service pursuant to what God has willed; with any remainder in what is personal to the ordinand, his purposeful renewal of self-dedication and the divine benediction upon him which the doing of this in sincerity always invokes? Or as hands are laid upon him and he hears, "Take thou authority to preach the Gospel," is something that is specially of God done or given?

Here again, as when we were speaking of the power of the Holy Spirit, the impression is with us that Church people have allowed themselves to be beguiled by an ideally-toned naturalism, or by what is really a pseudo-naturalism, into an indecision of thought whose "pale cast" over Ordination and other parts of the Church's

Order easily denudes them of vital quality. There is in all of us a disposition toward monism; reality is of one principle, hence spiritual states and happenings beneath their differentiating characters are subject with all else to law and sequential ordering. Imbued with this, we have come to expect from the moment of Ordination very little beyond what the assemblage of given and contrived conditions can be trusted to yield.

This, however, omits from the count the possibility of divine personal innovation. Whether or no it lies—as Kant believed—outside natural determinism, there is in man a freedom or power to innovate; one person can will changes in the experience of another and can act toward securing these changes. Can we deny a like freedom and power to God, only to His vaster measure? And may not God acting of His freedom also afford things to our experience, as an instance dispense His grace for our solace and strength, employing for this the occasion where we are assembled in expectation of it? Whence the reality of sacraments as acts of grace; they are such occasions for awaiting and expecting God's gracious action toward and within us. May not Ordination be another, so having at least in this aspect the character of a sacrament?

For revived certainty of the divine event in Ordination we need only to recover this freedom of God as against making Him the world's Process or constituent Principle; His freedom as the Personal God to will and do, as we being persons will and do to our restricted scale. The elements of Ordination are prayer and the laying on of hands; and one knows no cause for denying that God can—and does—in answer to the prayers of the Church and the ordinand's own prayer, bestow through the act of Ordination the special gift and grace for which Church and ordinand hope. Let the ordinand remember God's freedom, divine innovation even if he can think it only from the analogy of his own; let him be awake to God's power ministered through His Spirit, and then in the moment when he listens to "Take thou authority to preach" be trustful and expectant.

167

As in the sacrament of Communion, grace and blessing are dispensed to the believing worshipper, so the God who vouchsafes this can do this other: grant in Ordination a dispensation of the Gospel to him He has called to it and who in faith claims it, with authority to preach that Gospel.

What is this dispensation? We contested before the assumption that the Ministry of the Altar presupposes a higher enduement than the Ministry of the Word. It is as great a wonder to hear through human speech the Word of God as to behold Christ's corporeal reality in the sacramental elements. The Ministry of the Word rests on a miracle of divine power as truly as transubstantiation in the office of the Mass. The answer to our question then is: the dispensation of the Gospel that is given in Ordination is God's assurance to the one who is entering upon the Ministry of the Word that it shall be as He wills and as this Ministry requires: God will give and do that which takes his human word and makes it to those who receive it the divine testament to their souls. This is the meaning and fulfilment of Ordination in him who is being ordained: God pledging to him that which forms him as Minister and assures the divine acceptance of his work.

Thus the act of Ordination is no bare symbol; it is symbol instinct with the real. A symbolic act can be the thing it symbolizes. If one is uncertain of another's goodwill in an hour of anxiety, to meet that other and to receive a warm handclasp is to be reassured. The handclasp not only betokens the other's friendliness, but partakes of it and effectually imparts it. This is the force of symbol in Ordination, as of the forms and acts that symbolize Real Presence in sacramental worship. Christ is in the act as the kindliness of one's friend is in the handshake. In Ordination the ordinand reaches out to take the hand of God: *God takes his hand.* The laying on of hands is act or symbol with the Reality compact in the act.

This Reality is grace for the Ministry and the Spirit of truth and power. The gift of the Spirit in Ordination is to a Ministry meant, as we have seen, to be collaborator of the Spirit. This is the Ministry's true continuing: continuing

Ministry as the expression and function of the Holy Spirit in His continual striving for the ends of divine redemption, and in His steadfast upholding of the purpose and zeal of the Church as the sharer with Him of those ends.

v

The Ministry at Work Today

This book is not an essay in Practical or Pastoral Theology, hence under *The Ministry at Work* we shall not discuss the departments of the Minister's activity and methods or rules for effective service in them. The theme with which we have been occupied is the *Doctrine* of the Ministry, and this Doctrine as we have tried to discern it seeks the ground and purpose of the Ministry in God's activity of redemption in Jesus Christ and in the Gospel Word that brings assurance of this redemption to those whom God has invited to be the subjects of it. The Ministry is called and 'sent' to announce this Gospel, and empowered—by gift of God's own Power—to persuade men of its truth for them. Our consideration of *The Ministry at Work* will adhere to this; we shall glance at the Minister furbished with the Gospel message, and at the terms of his endeavour in enlightening and guiding the mind of our time in the realization of it.

The task of the Minister is to impress human society with this divine Gospel, and to make men esteem the Kingdom it opens to them as "the pearl of great price," the thing desirable and precious beyond all else. This is no light undertaking, for it involves the sweeping away of false estimations which find ends for man in material acquirement and in worldly and temporal security, honours and success. To light in men the vision that perceives their true good in the worship and righteousness of God, so that they become ready to part with all to obtain that good, is what the Minister seeks. The Minister's 'sights' are high who essays this, but nothing less is the requirement of his Gospel. Here we shall view the Minister working at this requirement amid the circumstances of contemporary life.

a. *The Minister Possesses a Gospel*

The title of this sub-section is an indicative. The Minister has a Gospel to proclaim. This is fact, or Church and Ministry—Christianity itself—are the mirage of human history.

It is an oft-repeated story how Karl Barth, ministering at Safenwil after the first world war, found his vocation as Minister—or was found of it—in divining it as not the giving of advice or discussing current questions as one versed in them, but as a prophesying under God to confront men with His Word and to lay it upon their hearts and wills. Christendom has had a shaking from this episode of Barth; it is always shaken, though the reverberations are seldom sensed as widely, when any Minister perceives His calling in the Gospel and consents to be made whole in dedication to it.

" His calling in the Gospel "—so the high pretension, not easy to elucidate or justify. Why should what is spoken by one person be Gospel to another, seeing it is a liability of all human speech to be fraught with error? We bring this liability to the reckoning in every other instance. Editors of newspapers, for example, may mould the thought of thousands, but subject to the will of each to criticize or contradict. Editors have no Word, however replete with wisdom their words. It has come to be that the preacher is similarly regarded; what he says may be received, but is as often rejected, ridiculed, ignored. Yet his is the Word, not words only, with the claim of the Word upon those who hear. The press has no claim save to share the common freedom of opinion and expression. The pulpit has the claim of its Message: not the voice of this or that preacher but truth from God borne and heard of them all, and sure and enduring as its Source.

This is the assertion of this present section, but have we a defence of it? Such as we shall offer lies in picturing certain of the conditions that are helpful and necessary to the

Minister's acquaintance with the divine Word and that being fulfilled go far to ensure his enduement with it.

A first condition is the lesson of several New Testament references. In Mk. 9 : 17-19, Jesus casts out a demonic spirit from a boy whose father had brought him to Him. The father had appealed to the disciples to cast the spirit out, but they could not. When Jesus did what His disciples had been unable to do, they asked why they were unable. His answer was, This kind can come forth by nothing but by prayer and fasting. The work of the Kingdom grows from a culture and regimen of the spirit that subdues natural inclination to it. In Acts 6 : 4, the Apostles desire relief from the service of tables to give themselves wholly to prayer and the Ministry of the Word. Prayer and this Ministry are not dual or collateral offices of Apostleship so much as effectual cause and consequent, as this order in naming them conveys. Prayer keeps the Ministry open toward its Source.

In another text, Acts 4 : 10-13, the Apostles' preaching of Jesus and the Resurrection causes men to 'marvel' and is the evidence to them that they, the preachers, have been with Jesus. So it has ever been: the preacher waits with his Master to receive the Word from Him and comes forth to proclaim it, not his own speculation or surmise. He studies —books for the freshening of his ideas—but more ardently the deep things of God in communion with the Spirit by whom they are searched and revealed (I Cor. 2 : 10); he studies that approved unto God he may rightly divide the Word (2 Tim. 2 : 15). This, then, we rank as a first requirement in the Minister, indispensable to his having the Gospel instinct with its rightful power: a propensity and discipline of the soul that orders him to Christ's own mind (our former "abiding in the Vine") and makes him meet to possess the Word in having become ready as its servant for full obedience to it.

Close to this first is a second necessity for the Minister who would make sure that the word he speaks is of God, not repetition or conjecture of his own. We spoke before of the babel that, as many hear, now sounds from the Church.

Where, they ask, is the one Word amid the clangour of incongruous versions of it, all equally confident that the truth is with them? The preacher answering this from his own judgment only adds one more to the general din. What this situation requires is of the same order as the former demand: as the Minister must commune daily with his Lord, so must he live with his Gospel, reaching ever deeper into it, constantly relearning and rediscovering it lest the forms that have been built about it hide it from him. By the nature of the Gospel as living Word, continually yielding things new and old, the Minister must cultivate eager and persisting discernment of those things, as his only defence against losing the Gospel or forgetting what it truly is.

The understanding Minister knows the urgency of this from his personal dilemmas. He easily drifts into presenting some one version of the Gospel, that is proving 'acceptable' to the people as well as to his own liking, and soon this version, again his own judgment or implicit valuation, is all he has to give; he becomes stolid and sterile in an 'interpretation' (or accommodation) of the Gospel as the Gospel itself would never allow him to be. The scribes and pharisees who make the Word of God of none effect by their tradition, who weave fabrics about the Word that then usurp its place, are a part of us all. Or there is the ever present danger to the Minister of self-deception in regard to his purpose and call. Recent psychology has confirmed what the religious analysts of the inner life have always seen, the power of less worthy motives to insinuate themselves among the higher ones while we assume the latter to be continuing uninterruptedly the governing role. The man who "wist not that the Lord was departed from him" (Judg. 16: 20) is at the head of a succession as truly as any Apostle. Against both of the pitfalls named in this paragraph a safeguard for the Minister is the continual learning of his Gospel of which we are thinking. It is the 'study' of 2 Tim. 2: 15 and the 'yoke' ("*learn of me*") of Mt. 11: 29. In this latter our two conditions, the Minister living with his Lord and with his Gospel, blend in one as is their real relation.

172

This oneness, the Minister's single and whole dedication to Christ and the Word, is his full security against the dangers we have been suggesting. It reverberated through the Church as only the truth can when the Jerusalem Meeting of the International Missionary Council (1928) made the same blend in its declaration: " Our Message *is* Jesus Christ." Nevertheless our separate mention of the two conditions, at this stage our stress on the need of study of the Gospel including the effort of the mind to understand, has justification in the ease with which we forget the place of this understanding in spiritual fulfilment, and in the mental sloth that is even flattered by this forgetting. The Minister's one choice against 'losing' his Gospel is his 'keeping' it as it is committed to him (I Tim. 6: 20); and this 'keeping' is not simply fastening to attention and memory its several items, but guarding it from perversion and debilitation through seeking more and more to apprehend and promulgate its richness and full consequence. The same word is used of Christ's 'keeping' that which His people have committed unto Him (2 Tim. 1: 12). The Minister possesses a Gospel and can never be dispossessed while he cherishes it as he himself is cherished and aspires to and loves its truth as he himself is loved.

This is possible to the Minister only through the divine working within him in the region of personal interaction where grace acts and faith answers. For the decisively formative thing in the Minister's preparation is the impact of God's redemption—the redemption he commends to others —on himself, his own spirit and conscience, whence he possesses the Gospel immediately in its energy and act and effect. Then he can witness, authoritatively, from personal constraint to the Authority of that to which he witnesses. The Minister possesses the Gospel to the degree of his possession by it.

b. The Minister Preaches the Gospel

Preaching the Gospel could be made to embrace the whole of the Minister's work. At the centre of that work is

173

Preaching in the specific sense. The Twelve were sent out to preach; the Risen Christ commands to preach to every creature, to teach all nations; God wills through "the foolishness of preaching" to save those who believe. But we do not need for the sake of Preaching to discount the conduct of worship or the pastoral ministry. There is no competition among the Minister's functions. Give Preaching its comprehension as the bringing of the Gospel to men for its fulfilment in them, and worship and the pastoral office are highest aids to it or of the substance of it. The sacraments among their other meanings are *verba visibilia*, words or the Word seen, by the side of Preaching specifically, the Word spoken and heard.

Preaching, then, can be depicted inclusively as the Minister's essential business. As such, keeping in mind the purpose of the Ministry, it is the instrument of God's great design in Christianity itself, the giving of His Word to the world with all that it brings to people here and now of hope for immortal good. This Word so directed to the world does two things: it reveals to the world the truth as to its need; it sets forth and proffers God's remedy for that need.

The Minister's success in preaching is to the measure of his making the world sensitive to these two ends of the Word: alive to its true need and responsive to God's offer in answer to it. The task this implies is prodigious, wholly beyond human accomplishment. We shall glance at this task in the order implied by these two aims of the Word.

Faring forth on the first, the uncovering of the world's actual need, the Preacher today faces a lowering cloudbank of blindness and complacency. Complacency derives from blindness; it is self-satisfaction from illusion of the actuality of that which of its quality is deemed a proper cause of satisfaction. The subject believes he is enlightened and clothed upon with sincerity and goodness; and—as the Laodiceans—knows not that he is naked and blind, self-deluded and inadequate to the time's real issues and demands.

Who shall say this is not the affliction of our culture and age? The Western world has had "the oracles of God"; it has been the home of the Christian tradition. It has also more than other regions experienced the transformations accruing from the scientific and industrial revolutions. Small wonder if we of the West feel that on us the ends of the world have come; it is ours to light the way for the nations. Our own wellbeing is abundant, and if we have problems, our resource and purpose are more than a match for them.

But the question Christianity bids us ask is whether these comfortable notions about our state and capability arise from true self-knowledge. Have we stopped to examine if what we think of ourselves accords with what God thinks of us? The Rich Fool of the parable (Lk. 12: 16-21) was self-adulatory over his success, but God's assessment of his case was very different. Our system of life on this North American continent is one whose very complexity makes extraordinarily hazardous the attempt to discern where the line falls between what God would approve and what He would not. Human complaisance and egotism can usually be trusted in such an *impasse* to set under credit much whose proper place is the other scale. The Preacher whose plumbline is the Word of God has here a trenchant challenge. Few things would serve better our common life and restore fibre to our Christian profession than a quickened perception of what in our accepted behaviour receives God's judgment rather than His favour; in other words, a renewed conviction of sin, only 'conviction' having its instigation not from traditional notions of sin so much as from our actual personal and communal sinning. The Word of God brings conviction of sin in fulfilling its first office, revealing to men their need; man's need of what God offers in the Gospel being on account of sin. The Preacher in possessing the Gospel is the agent of this conviction; he has for our age no greater ministry than that which belongs to this first phase in ministering the Word: to lead men to that self-understanding which shatters spurious self-content in making them alive to that state

175

of themselves by reason of which the Gospel is spoken to them.

Then the second office of the Word: to bring to men's state and need, God's remedy. What mood does the Preacher encounter who essays this? Sophisticated man can be as deluded about the cure for his malady as about its nature; he will be the one in being the other. Superficial self-diagnosis betrays one to the lure of the easy answer. People can beguile themselves regarding progress in things spiritual as in other spheres. Currently a religious revival is astir in North America, or, as much hopeful rumour has it, in most of the world. What is the tenor of this revival? Is this continent being gripped anew at its heart by the dynamic Verities of Faith? Are the dominant powers of our civilization reaching out for God's way purposefully and resolvedly as heretofore they have not done? Some of the sociologists express doubts; " is it," they ask, " merely peace of mind which a restless, speed-possessed, frightened world is seeking? " Is it, the Preacher can ask, a vaguely theistic outlook to which men are turning, easily embraced and to those who crave ephemeral consolation promising quick returns? These are some of the questions the Minister examines and brings to the standard of God's measure of the people's fears and hopes and His provision for them. The Minister is not cynical; he owns much good in contemporary religious attitudes and aspirations. But he sets over them the fulness of the Word in judgment and promise. He is confident in no deliverance from mankind's perplexities, save God's deliverance.

Reinhold Niebuhr has written: "We cannot deny the indictment that we seek a solution for practically every problem of life in quantitative terms; and are not fully aware of the limits of this approach."[1] The Preacher of the New Testament Gospel has here his mandate. That we have advanced beyond other peoples in the area of the material is our spiritual Nemesis if it snares us into seeing and esteeming all else in the light of it. The possibility of our slipping into this valuation makes the preaching of the Gospel as

[1] *The Irony of American History*, p. 59.

crucial a necessity for our condition and age as it has ever or anywhere been.

Our brief discussion of *The Ministry at Work* has had in prospect our day and our own world. This is for verisimilitude; the Gospel is for every day and place, but its impact is always upon the "here and now", the eternal Word in the given situation. Its truth is for all situations; our discussion in the reference of one has *mutatis mutandis* universal applicability. But the universal becomes effectual for us—for all people severally—in the idiom of the particular; the Word that is from the beginning is seen with *our* eyes (I John 1: 1). The Minister does not take his Gospel from the communal and cultural order about him, but he does bring his Gospel to it in the expression the effective doing of this demands. This done by each Minister, the Gospel is by the whole Ministry brought to all: God's one Word is preached to the world.

Summary

I DON'T know if it is good practice in teaching Systematic Theology to give, at the end of a section devoted to one of the areas of doctrine, a summary statement of what has been attempted. On the one hand, it may seem like trying to wrap in a formula what ought still to live and move. On the other, a summary may provide a review that may serve to restore acquaintance with the intended direction of the thought that has been given.

At the end of this book, which has been occupied with a division of doctrine, I feel it is the second consideration that carries the weight. This is because the book will meet in many minds the charge of inconsistency, or of trying to teach two disparate doctrines in one. The writer would claim it doesn't do this; but he owns it may easily so seem and offers this summary in part against this seeming.

The summary may recall first a major note of the book that the writer trusts escapes this charge in being quite un-equivocal. It is that the Church's Ministry is not a mere human or ecclesiastical expedient; it is of the will of God, out of the depths of His purpose, that the Ministry has come to be. Christ chose Ministers for His Church and He con-tinues to choose and ordain. The Church chooses, prepares and ordains conformably to the will of Christ and as guided by His Spirit.

It is when we come to specific forms of Ministry that the argument of the book can appear self-contradictory. Does it favour the claims of Episcopacy or does it not? The first part of the book builds a case for Episcopacy, for its primacy among Ministries. Episcopacy has the strong sanction of history and of a consensus of Christian testimony. But the book then proceeds to a criticism which, not invalidating

Episcopacy, withholds from it any necessity or essential character not shared by other Ministries.

The explanation is this: and it touches what I believe to be basic in the examination of the Ministry. History is to be regarded, not as a flux of characterless happenings, but as achievement. Christianity in history is not something placed there full-orbed to go on without change. Christianity in part *becomes* through history. Having had a history, there is a historical component in the present being of it. England, to take another case, existed in the time of Edward I, but today, because of what has since transpired, there is much in the connotation of England, much wrought into the very being of England, that had no place in that earlier time. Similarly Christianity can be thought of as historically formed, as well as given or inserted at a point in history.

Now there is an argument for regarding Episcopacy as substantially belonging to this historically constituted Christianity. There have been non-episcopal expressions of Christianity; some, as in the Reformed Churches, of great historical prominence. But from the early centuries, widely if not on the whole, Episcopacy has been a part of the Christian fabric in the world, to a degree that makes it not unreasonable now to regard it as of the being of historical Christianity.

Hence it is, not practical Church politics (we are not thinking of that), but only historical realism or conformity to high historical probability to augur for the Episcopal Ministry an active place in Christianity's world future. A united Christendom to be non-episcopal would have to undo much of its formative history. It is fidelity to history, to Christianity as historically fashioned, to view Episcopacy as germane to corporate Christianity and entitled to continue as a major Ministry. All this is no more than to be factual concerning Christianity as an accomplishment of history.

But as well as Christianity historically ordered, there is Christianity in its pristine inalienable nature. That Episcopacy—or any form of Ministry or Order—is a part of the historical composite of Christianity does not involve its necessary derivation from Christianity's pristine or essential being. Christianity in its absolute or aboriginal essence is neither episcopal nor non-episcopal. By the standard of historical predominance, non-episcopal ministries are unequal to the episcopal; but by absolute Christian criteria, a non-episcopal ministry can be as genuine, as characteristically Christian, as an episcopal, and has often conspicuously so been.

The apparent contradiction in our treatment of Episcopacy in this book comes of the presence of these two strands in Christian judgment. Under the one, Episcopacy in the way just stated has a precedence of other Ministries, but it stands on common ground with them before the other. Christianity was in the world before the rise of Episcopacy; yet having regard to the creative instrumentality of history and what has accrued to Christianity from it, who could now dispense with Episcopacy in thinking Christianity's world position? It is this vital conjunction of Episcopacy with history, not its identity with originals "beyond history"[1] (to which other Ministries may lie as close), that is the true appeal of the "Historic Episcopate". This appeal counsels the inclusion of Episcopacy in plans for Church reunification, not to smooth the way in union negotiations, but from the right and duty to continue a great historic and historically established Ministry. Maintaining Episcopacy is of principle, not just convenience; but principle having its fibre not so much from Christianity in its pure definition as from the actualizations of Christian history.

Deeper than this, however, is the application of the pure and primary Christian tests to all Christian Ministries. For our two standards in Christian judgment are not equal; primary or essential Christianity is the norm even for *criteria* derived from history. The two standards are confused when Episcopacy, seen as of the being of Christianity historically, is regarded without further token as of it essentially, of its *esse*. The tests of essential Christianity are for the validation of all Ministries that possess their office

[1] Cf. *Lambeth Conference, 1920 (supra,* p. 29).

under the dictum, not now of patterns of history, but of the given and perfect Word of Christ. Episcopacy has the weight of history to justify designating it the Church's 'regular' Ministry, but this imports nothing as to its superior quality or authenticity. Other Ministries with a lesser role in history, minor and humble Ministries, are *basically* just as authentic if established in the Word.

Thus the Doctrine of the Ministry outlined in this book commends these two: upholding Episcopacy with its claims as they arise from the fashion in which Christianity from its truth and in its rightful historical course has come to be; eschewing along with this all thought of deficiency—certainly to the degree calling for re-ordination—in other Ministries that by Christianity's essential dicta are genuine Ministries. Re-ordination would be repugnant to the principles of this book in all cases where first ordination constituted a true Gospel Ministry.

Indexes

Index of Scripture References

OLD TESTAMENT

	PAGE		PAGE
Exodus		*1 Kings*	
12:38	49, 77	17:1-5	163
19:5, 6	42		
24:1	74	*2 Kings*	
28:1	139, 162	2:9	163
28:1, 40, 41, 43	161	2:12	163
Leviticus		*Psalms*	
19:18	45	22:22	41
Numbers		*Isaiah*	
1	78, 82	53	43, 44
1:1-17	45, 48	61:1	134
11	77, 78, 80, 82		
11:4	49, 77	*Jeremiah*	
11:4, 5	77	1:5	162
11:16	74, 78	7:25, 26	52
11:17	77, 165		
11:4-17	48, 77	*Ezekiel*	
		8:11	74
Deuteronomy			
6:4, 5	45	*Joel*	
		2:28-32	132
Judges			
16:20	172	*Amos*	
		7:14, 15	162
1 Samuel			
15:1	52		

NEW TESTAMENT

	PAGE
Matthew	
5:22	75
7:29	158
10:1-7	40
10:2, 5, 19, 20, 40	52
10:5, 6	49
10:5-8	126
10:7	50, 117, 126
10:17	75
10:20	155
11:27	102
11:29	152, 172
16:16, 17	51
16:17	102
16:18	127
16:19	50, 69, 103, 156, 158
18:18	69
19:28	44, 46
22:37-39	45
23:1-12	129
28:16-20	128
28:18	158
28:18, 19	102
28:18-20	15, 103
28:19	132, 152
28:19, 20	54
28:20	132, 133
Mark	
1:11	47
1:15	43
2:10	54
3:7-14	40
3:13, 14	117
3:14	50
3:14, 15	126
3:14-19	46

	PAGE
Mark (cont.)	
9:7	102
9:17-19	171
9:35	159
10:38, 39	156
10:43, 44	129
10:45	43, 146
13:9	75
13:10	97, 132
16:14-18	128
16:15	50, 132
Luke	
1:2	81
4:16-21	44
4:18	134
8:1	50
9:1	15, 54, 62, 78, 150, 157
9:1, 2	151
9:1-6	40
9:2	50, 117, 126
9:2, 6	126, 127
10	78
10:1	48, 49, 78
10:16	52
10:17	49
11:52	157
12:16-21	175
16:16	44
22:19	151
22:26	159
22:27	150
22:30	44, 46
22:32	55
22:37	44
24:49	132, 137

PAGE

PAGE

John

Acts (cont.)

1 : 1	114
1 : 13	149
1 : 14	23
1 : 18	102
5 : 30	52
7 : 39	133
13 : 35	30
14 : 10	52
14 : 16, 26	132
14 : 17	103, 133
14 : 18-20	132
14 : 26	133
15	150
15 : 4, 7	152
15 : 15	52
15 : 16	130
15 : 26	102, 134
15 : 26, 27	102, 103, 133
16 : 12	98
16 : 13	98
16 : 13, 14	133, 155
17 : 23	52
17 : 25	102
20 : 19-23	128
20 : 21	52
20 : 21-23	50, 137
20 : 21, 23	69
20 : 22	23
20 : 23	103, 156, 158
21 : 15-17	128

Acts

1 : 2-8	128
1 : 4-8	137
1 : 8	103, 132, 133, 134
1 : 15-26	56
2 : 1-18	132
2 : 4	134
2 : 33	132

2 : 42	65, 68, 81, 97, 98, 117, 128
2 : 47	128
3 : 1	141
3 : 12, 25, 26	42
4 : 2	126
4 : 10-13	171
5 : 32	103, 134
5 : 42	126
6	149, 150
6 : 1	76, 77
6 : 1-6	75, 77, 78, 80, 81, 84
6 : 2	76
6 : 2, 4	127
6 : 2, 5	77
6 : 3	78, 81, 149
6 : 3, 5, 6	81
6 : 4	76, 78, 81, 99, 117, 171
6 : 6	58
6 : 7	139
6 : 9–8 : 1	78
7 : 38	41
8	76
8 : 4	126
9 : 4-6, 15	57
9 : 13-15	162
9 : 17, 18	162
11 : 1	81
11 : 29, 30	80
11 : 30	81
13	139, 150
13 : 1, 2	139, 162
13 : 1-3	57, 162
13 : 2	140
13 : 2, 3	149
14 : 14	81
14 : 14, 23	58, 79
14 : 23	63, 79, 80, 116

PAGE

Acts (cont.)

15	64
15:1-25	57
15:2, 6, 22, 23	74, 81, 84
16:1-3	57
17:18	126
20:17	80
20:17, 28	59, 80
20:28	59, 122
21:8	76
22:20	102

Romans

1:1, 16	129
1:4	102
5:19	146
8:9-11	134
12:1	140, 143, 146
12:4-8	117
12:5, 6	116
15:16	143, 146

1 Corinthians

1:1	56, 117
1:21, 23	23
2:4, 5	134
2:7-10	155
2:7-11	133
2:10	102, 171
3, 12	150
7:11	156
9:1	57, 73
9:1, 2	56
9:16	130
9:19	129
12:1-11	117
12:3	102
12:4, 5	138
12:4,7	116
12:7	138
12:28	13, 117, 122, 126

PAGE

1 Corinthians (cont.)

12:31	116
15:3	57, 117
15:8	57

2 Corinthians

2:10	54, 69, 103
5:18	158
5:19, 20	131
5:20	54

Galatians

1:1	57, 129, 162
1:8	65, 97
1:15	162
1:15-17	56
1:18, 19	56
2:20	54
3:13, 14, 16, 17, 29	42

Ephesians

2:20	70, 100
3, 4	150
4:11	14, 117, 122, 133
4:11, 12	126
4:11-13	30, 117
4:12, 13	133

Philippians

1:1	59, 63, 77, 84, 117

1 Thessalonians

2:10	102

1 Timothy

1:2	57
1:3	57, 66, 67, 149
2:7	66
3	77, 84
3:1	59

	PAGE
1 Timothy (cont.)	
3 : 1-8	59
3 : 1-13	149
3 : 8-13	58, 117
4 : 14	8, 149
5 : 1-5	117
5 : 4, 16	59
6 : 3	59
6 : 20	66, 117, 173
2 Timothy	
1 : 2	57
1 : 6	58
1 : 12	173
2 : 2	57, 58, 66, 67, 117, 133, 162
2 : 14	133, 157
2 : 15	149, 171, 172
4 : 3	66
4 : 5	148
4 : 21	67
Titus	
1 : 4	57
1 : 5	57, 58, 79, 80, 81, 116
1 : 5-7	59, 60
1 : 5-9	80, 149
1 : 6	59
Hebrews	
1 : 3	145, 147
2 : 12	41
5 : 7-9	145
7 : 21-24	139

	PAGE
Hebrews (cont.)	
7 : 25	145
7 : 26	148
7 : 27	145, 147
8 : 1-6	143, 144
8 : 2	139
9 : 28	144
10 : 1, 9	128
10 : 5, 7	144
10 : 9	47
10 : 10	144
10 : 12	144
12 : 2	145
1 Peter	
2 : 9	23, 139
2 : 5, 9	42
5 : 1-5	80
5 : 3	150
1 John	
4 : 17	53
2 John	80
3 John	80
vv. 9, 10	60, 64
Revelation	
1 : 6	116, 139, 140
2	60
3	60
3 : 14	102
14 : 6	97
22 : 17	116

General Index

Baillie, D. M., 8, 33, 93
Barth, K., 170
Book of Common Prayer, 11
Brunner, E., 159
Bulgakov, S., 17, 19
Bultmann, R., 44

Calvin, J., 70, 71
Casserley, J. V. L., 90, 91
Catholic and Reformed Ministries Compared, 151-56
I Clement, 62, 63, 71
Cullman, O., 119
Cyprian, 70, 76

Davies, R. E., 114, 115, 125
Didache, 59, 71, 140
Didascalia Apostolorum, 68, 71
Dix, G., 15, 36, 82
Dodd, C. H., 98

Ehrhardt, A., 116, 130
Evanston Assembly, World Council of Churches, 93

Fairweather, E. R., 12, 15, 16, 20, 22, 107
Farrar, A. M., 77
Flew, R. N., 43, 114, 115, 116, 125
Florovsky, G., 93
Forsyth, P. T., 25, 28, 111

Garbett, C. F., 34, 68, 90, 101

Gnosis, Gnosticism, 65, 66
Gore, C., 13, 20, 21, 23, 24

Hebert, A. G., 143
Hegesippus, 65
Hettlinger, R. F., 15, 16, 22, 107
Hippolytus, 69, 70, 71, 82
Hodgson, L., 31, 32, 33
Hooker, R., 11, 12, 26, 76

Ignatius, 60, 61, 62, 71, 84
Iremonger, F. A., 26
Irenaeus, 20, 66, 67, 68, 71, 92, 94, 96, 111-14

Jalland, T. G., 59
Jenkins, D., 28
Johnson, A. R., 51
Josephus, 74, 75, 80
Justin Martyr, 84

Keble, J., 27
Kirk, K. E., 9, 21, 73, 142
Knox, W. L., 27, 33, 86, 87

Lacey, T. A., 13, 14, 70
Lambeth Conference, 1920, 29, 73, 181
Lambeth Conference, 1930, 20, 31
Lausanne Conference on Faith and Order, 1927, 7
Lietzmann, H., 127
Life and Liberty Movement, 26
Lubac, H. de, 17, 18, 19

Manson, T. W., 125, 130
Marsh, J., 8, 33, 93
Maurice, F. D., 36
Methodist Recorder, Jan. 6, 1956, 24
Micklem, N., 7

Neill, S., 119, 164
Niebuhr, Reinhold, 176

Ordination, 166-69

Pauck, W., 33
Pittenger, W. N., 14, 19, 107, 108
Potter, J., 12, 13
Priestly Absolution, 103, 156-58

Quick, O. C., 31

Reformation, 35
Roman Catholic Ordinal, 82, 83

Sanday, W., 97
Schweitzer, A., 39
Scott, J., 12
Shaliach, 51-55, 102, 130, 131
Simpson, Carnegie, 18, 19
Streeter, B. H., 43

Temple, F., 24, 25, 90
Temple, W., 7, 13, 24, 26
Thornton, L. S., 36
Tillich, P., 119
Torrance, T. F., 141
Toynbee, A., 106
Tractarian Movement, 27
Transubstantiation, 151-56

Van de Pol, W. H., 17, 19

James T. Burtchaell.   CUP
The Synagogue & Church.   1992

Was the Early Church dominated by ordained
ministers or the 'Charismata'.
Burtchaell starts with Judaism. — He sees the
evidence in favour of the Catholic/orthodox/Anglican
view that Bishops have always presided in the
Christian Church. At the same time He argues alongside
the Protestant that in its formative era the Church
deferred most to the judgement of those who were
inspired yet never ordained. (Earlier — I thought that
two years ago!)
There is no ancient precedent which by itself
legitimises any contemporary polity.
Look at all the evidence. Episcopacy at first a stopgap
evidence. Episcopacy at first a stopgap
effort. Always there the disintegration of a community's
organization. The consensus that the Church
has all been is really undermined.
Burtchaell looks at all the recent books from
from the Reformation onwards.

Survey of Wyclif. Luther. Calvin. Puritans.
Pietists et al.

Crit. Consensus. Rothe, Ritschl, Lightfoot, Hatch.

Harnack. Sohm — Very anti-Catholic — no real diff. at all.

Anti-canon styles :- Kirk's fine speech :- Flew. Manson's Jarrett.

Manson enters the Kirk — dix lin c. Schweizer.

Von Campenhausen, Schillebeeckx — Elisabeth

Schüssler Fiorenza who says it always patriarchal.

Jeretchlark does not mention numbers or Crises —

Telfer only occurs in a footnote !!

Synagogue — the Elders. Senior Elder. Government

women ambivalent — Wives.

Faith & Mother the synagogue Sanhe.

Much of the Synagogue survives into Christianity.

Jeretchlark makes a strong case though not a

Complete one I think.

There could be a President & a charismatic

activist — Just as Mother Teresa was a minister!

It is as if once more what Paul & Clement

and Ignatius as the Didache & their contemporaries

taught was a return Koja ; that

episcope = presbytery Could be diakonias

service & hegemonia = governance Could be

a letourgia = public service = if

pneumatikoi = inspired people were

chosen as the presbyteroi = elders.

Jeretchlark for a strong case but strangely

ignores Telfer's Crisis view as the writings of

Jarrett in this area but then don't Litchko
                                          thesis.

T. M. Lindsay.

The Church and the Ministry in the Early
Centuries   Hodder 1901.   PP398.

Written when Lindsay was Principal
of the Glasgow College of the United Free Church
Scotland). Following Hatch rather than Gore.
Nonspirited organization Necessary. By it 'from above
or from below'. There may be a ministerial priesthood
but there cannot be a Mediatize priesthood within the
christian society. P. 35.   Apostle, prophet, Teachers.
The organization of Bishop, deacon of Elders & the board
Deacons became almost universal within the Empire
Downfall of Prophetic ministry. (3 church to priesthood
Conception.   A fine piece of work overshadowed by
Charles Gore unfortunately

The Much Neglected Edwin Hatch is worth
Noting also.
E. Hatch. The Organization of the
Early Christian churches. 8 lectures delivered
before the university of Oxford in the Year 1880.
                                        Bampton
2nd W. Rivingtons. 1882   Lectures.